Eight Decades in Syria

Eight Decades in Syria

by A.J. McFarland

WESTPHALIA PRESS
An imprint of Policy Studies Organization

Eight Decades in Syria

Westphalia Press
An imprint of Policy Studies Organization
1527 New Hampshire Ave., NW
Washington, D.C. 20036
dgutierrezs@ipsonet.org

ISBN-13: 978-1935907565
ISBN-10: 1935907565

Updated material and comments on this edition
can be found at the Westphalia Press website:
www.westphaliapress.org

EIGHT DECADES IN SYRIA

by A. J. McFARLAND, D. D.

New Inkzik Church, dedicated November 15, 1936

FOREWORD

In response to a demand for information and factual material that may be used in study groups throughout the church the Board of Foreign Missions has undertaken to publish a series of booklets to meet that need. This is the second in that series. The first was a brief history of the work of the Covenanter Church in South China. This is a resume of the work begun and carried on for a period of eighty years in North Syria. The compiler and writer of this brief history is the Rev. A. J. McFarland, D. D., who went out as a missionary in the year 1906 *after a ten year pastorate in the homeland. He is still in active service in* 1936.

The story covers the work of our Scotch-Irish brethren in the Alexandretta-Antioch district just north of the Latakia province. These are two parts of one field where the missionaries of the Scotch-Irish and American Covenanter Church work together in harmony with a free interchange of ideas and workers as the needs of the field as a whole demand. It also records the extension of the work into Cilicia in Asia Minor. The American Board of the Congregational Church had a flourishing work among the Armenians in the Turkish language as they had also in a few places in North Syria. The line of demarcation was that of language. Our work was in Arabic among the Arabic-speaking populations in both Syria and Cilicia. Thus the work in the Levant was marked by a unity until the Church ventured into Cyprus into quite a different language and different type of population whose interests were with the West rather than with the East, with Greece rather than with Syria. This development seems to have been accidental rather than a step forward as part of a reasoned and thought out program. But that is another story of which we shall hear more later.

The roster of missionaries to this field is a long one and contains many distinguished names. The soil of Syria, like that of South China, is hallowed for here lies the dust of the honored dead. The names of Robert James Dodds, David

Metheny, Emma Gregg Metheny. Archibald Dodds, Mattie R. Wylie, Robert E. Willson, May Elsey, Maggie Edgar, and Elma French will long be remembered.

Some regard Syria as a comparatively barren and unfruitful field. They are forgetful of the vicissitudes through which that field has passed. They are unmindful of the toll taken by a steady stream of emigration to other lands on account of intolerable economic and political conditions; of massacres, forced deportations, and war that have devastated that fair land and which might have completely discouraged less stout-hearted workers. The wonder is not that there is so little to show but that the work is as promising as it is.

This little book is sent out in the hope that it will stimulate interest and draw out a more continuous prayer support for this field that has been so dear to the heart of the Covenanter Church.

THE COVENANTER MISSION FIELD OF NORTH SYRIA

Roster of Missionaries

TERMS OF SERVICE

(AMERICAN)

Rev. and Mrs. Robert J. Dodds....................................1856-1870
Rev. and Mrs. Joseph Beattie.......................................1856-1883
Rev. David Metheny, M. D...1865-1897
Mrs. Emma Gregg Metheny...1865-1876
Miss Rebecca Crawford...1867-1879
(Mrs. James Martin)
Rev. S. R. Galbraith..1872-1872 (Died)
Mrs. S. R. Galbraith..1872-1872
Miss Mary Ellen Dodds...1872-1877
(Married Dr. Metheny)
Rev. and Mrs. Henry Easson.......................................1873-1892
Miss Mattie R. Wylie...1875-1916
Rev. and Mrs. W. J. Sproull..1879-1886
Miss Mary E. Carson...1879-1880
Dr. Archibald Dodds...1881-1885
Miss Evadna Sterrett...1881-1919
(Mrs. Balph, 1919-1926)
Miss Meta Cunningham...1883-1906
Miss Maggie B. Edgar...1886-1932
Miss Lillian Joseph...1887-1892
Miss Willa Dodds..1887-1904
Dr. James M. Balph...1887-1926
Mrs. James M. Balph...1887-1892
Rev. and Mrs. James S. Stewart..................................1888-1920
Rev. and Mrs. R. J. Dodds...1890-1907
Mrs. Mary McCarroll...1890-1892
(Mrs. J. S. Crawford)
Rev. J. Boggs Dodds....................................1893-1903, 1906-1908
Mrs. Myrta May Dodds...1893-1903
Miss Jennie B. Dodds..1893-1897
(Mrs. S. H. Kennedy)
Dr. and Mrs. W. M. Moore..1893-1896
(Cyprus 1896-1903)
Miss Lizzie McNaughton...1893-1903
Dr. and Mrs. S. A. S. Metheny....................................1896-1900
Mrs. Peenlope Allen Balph..1896-1913
Rev. and Mrs. C. A. Dodds...1898-1908
Rev. and Mrs. A. J. McFarland.....................................1906-
Miss Zada Patton..1906-1910
(Mrs. J. D. Edgar)
Rev. Samuel Edgar...................................1907-1915; 1918-1921

Mrs. Samuel Edgar....1907-1915
Dr. John Peoples....1907-1920
Mrs. John Peoples....1910-1917
Miss F. Elma French....1907-1914, 1919-1934
Rev. R. E. Willson....1908-1913, 1919-1923 (Died)
Mrs. R. E. Willson....1908-1913, 1919-1923
Miss Florence May Elsey....1908-1913
Miss Anna Louise Crockett....1910-1914
Miss Florence Mearns....1913-1915
Mr. J. French Carrithers....1913-1917
Miss Annie L. Kennedy....1920-1926
Dr. and Mrs. R. Esmond Smith....1921-1934
Miss Mary E. Shanks....1920-1921
Miss Elizabeth McElroy....1920-
Miss Agnes M. Archer....1922-1923
(Mrs. Wm. Lytle)
Miss Lillian Cunningham....1922-1927
Mr. and Mrs. Chester T. Hutcheson....1928-
Miss Reah J. McElroy....1926-1931
Miss Rose A. Huston....1927-1928
Rev. and Mrs. Herbert A. Hays....1935-

(BRITISH)

Rev. James Martin....1872-1924
Mrs. James Martin....1872-1877
Mrs. Rebecca Crawford Martin....1879-1896
Mrs. Linehart Martin....1900-1924
Miss Linehart....1900-1924
Miss Evangeline Metheny....1904-1935
Rev. S. H. Kennedy....1895-
Mrs. Jennie B. Kennedy....1897-
Rev. William Lytle....1919-
Miss M. K. Cunningham....1920-
Miss M. E. G. Houston....1921-1923 (Died)
Mrs. Agnes Archer Lytle....1923-
Miss Emily Lytle....1927-1931
Miss Muriel Russell....1931-
Rev. Archibald Guthrie....1934-

Hayti

PORT AU PRINCE. At the meeting of Synod in 1818, a Committee was appointed to inquire into the expediency of establishing a Foreign Mission. Nothing was done, however, until 1841, when a memorial from the brethren of the Philadelphia congregation led to the approval of the plan, and, at the meeting in 1843, a Committee was appointed to select a field for operations. In 1845, the Island of St. Thomas was chosen, but the following year abandoned, and Hayti was selected. In the fall of 1846, the Rev. J. B. Johnston was sent out by the Board to inspect the field, and Port au Prince was designated as the center of operations. In May, 1847, the Rev. J. W. Morton and A. M. Milligan, licentiate, were chosen Missionaries. Mr. Milligan declined, and Mr. R. J. Dodds, student of theology, was chosen. In the fall of 1847, Mr. Morton, with his family, repaired to the scene of his labors at Port au Prince. After preparing himself, and some books in the French language, he opened a successful school. While laboring there, Mr. Morton changed his views with reference to the Christian Sabbath, denying that the first day of the week was such. He returned to lay his case before Synod, and was suspended in May, 1849. The Mission was then abandoned, and Mr. Dodds was not sent out.

THE RELATION OF
Our Mission Field
TO
SOUTHERN SYRIA, EGYPT,
ETC.
Scale of Statute Miles
KONIA
ADANA
ALEPPO
SYRIA
CYPRUS
MEDITERRANEAN SEA
EGYPT
ARABIA
Konia
Iconium
Bey shehr
Lystra
Eregli
Derbe
Karaman
TAURUS MOUNTAINS
Guzney
Tarsus
Adana
MERSINA
Mut
Erdemli
Alaja
Selefke
C. Lisan et Khbe
C. Anemour
Sis
R. Jihan
Marash
Bay of Alexandretta
Alexandretta
ALEPPO
SUADIA
ANTIOCH
Idlib
Kessab
Inkzik
C. St. Andrea
Jendairia
Gunaimia
LATAKIA
Merj
Al Daibey
Bahamra
Jebley
C St Epiphamos
Kerinia
Famagusta
Troodos
Nicosia
LARNACA
Limasol
C. Gatta
Banias
HAMATH
Bizak
Soda
Metn
Tartoos
Melket
HUMS
TRIPOLI
LEBANON
ANTI LEBANON
Beyrout
BAALBEC
Sidon
DAMASCUS
Tyre
MT HERMON
Banias
Acre
Capernaum
MT CARMEL
Sea of Galilee
Nazareth
Tiberias
Cæsarea
Beisan
Samaria
R. Jordan
Shechem
Joppa, Jaffa
JERUSALEM
Jericho
Ashkelon
Bethlehem
Hebron
DEAD SEA
Gaza
Beersheba
To Alexandria
90 Statute Miles
Damietta
NILE
Port Said
Suez Canal

Eight Decades in Syria

THE BEGINNINGS OF OUR WORK

Barring abortive attempts to start work in the West Indies, the Foreign Mission work of the Covenanter Church of America really began in 1856, when four young missionaries with Christian faith and courage responded to the call of God through His Church, in the meeting of Synod that year, and braved the hardships of separation from dear friends and the home land, the perils of a long and weary journey over six thousand miles of ocean, and life in a new and untried country under the uncertain protection of the then Turkish government, in order to carry the Gospel of Light and Salvation to the people long sitting in darkness in Syria.

THE TIME PROPITIOUS

The time, the place and the persons were well chosen. The Crimean War had just ended. Turkey had been wrested from the deadly embrace of the Russian Bear by the British and French and saved from a "be nevolent assimilation" by Russia, which would have made Turkey as inaccessible to Protestant missionaries as Russia has always been. British and, incidentally, American prestige in Turkey were thus greatly increased, an dour missionaries found access to the country less difficult than it might otherwise have been.

Also the Rev. Samuel Lyde of the Anglican Church had labored against great odds to establish a small mission for the Nusairiyeh or Alaweets at Bahamra, a small village in the province of Latakia, but had reached the end of his strength on account of the unusual hardships he had endured. At one time he was yoked up with a donkey and made to draw a light native plow operated by one of his persecutors. He was quite ready to hand over his work to our pioneers on their arrival, thus leaving the whole province of Latakia to us as an open field for Protestant work. He died the following year in Egypt.

THE PERSONNEL WELL SUITED

As to the persons, their lives and ministry are a complete vindication of the wisdom of their appointment.

ROBERT JAMES DODDS

Rev. Robert James Dodds, accorded the degree of D. D. in 1870, had been pastor of a "backwoods" congregation of six societies scattered over the pine clad hills of three counties in Western Pennsylvania, Armstrong, Clarion and Jefferson. It was called Rehoboth Congregation "because they had plenty of room." His parish was forty-five miles long by thirty miles wide, so he spent much of his time on horseback to cover it all. But such was his untiring zeal that in the four years prior to his call to Syria he built up a number of flourishing stations there. He thus served an excellent apprenticeship for the task before him in Syria. He is described as "a remarkably cheerful man, uniform in his dealings and sympathetic in his disposition, with keen and vigorous reasoning powers."

He buried his first wife, Amanda Cannon, in a lonely country cemetery in Jefferson County, Pennsylvania. His two motherless children he left with his father, thus early experiencing one of the sorest trials of the foreign missionary, the separation from his small children. Just before sailing he married Letitia M. Dodds, who bore him seven children. He died at Allepo, Syria, December 11, 1870, after only two years of work there, nine years in Latakia and three years in the Lebanons, making fourteen in all. It was a rich ministry and productive of much fruit.

MRS. LETITIA M. DODDS

Mrs. Letitia M. Dodds was of a serene and quiet disposition but an excellent wife and mother. Her seven children left fatherless at an early age have given abundant witness by their lives to her wise and faithful devotion to their best interests. She was one of those women whose price is above rubies. Her children arise up and call her blessed. Strength and honor are her clothing and she shall rejoice in time to come.

JOSEPH BEATTIE

Rev. Joseph Beattie, given her degree of D. D. in 1878, had just been licensed to preach by Philadelphia Presbytery when he received the call to Syria. He was ordained *sine titulo* by New York Presbytery before his departure for his field of service. He was married about the same time to Martha E. Lord who accompanied him.

Mr. Beattie was a man of fine appearance, rich Christian experience and sound judgment. He was a faithful minister of the Gospel, a judicious teacher and one generally beloved for his kindness and sympathy. He did yeoman service in establishing the Syrian Mission, which he served for twenty-seven years until his death in October, 1883. A goodly number were brought to Christ through his ministry.

MRS. MARTHA E. BEATTIE

Mrs. Martha E. Beattie, his wife, seems to have been the least rugged of this quartette of pioneers, although high testimonials are given of her Christian graces and consecration to the service. Four children were born to her and buried in infancy during the first eight years of their sojourn in Syria. Finally, impaired health and the necessity of educating the other children seemed to make it wise for her to return to the home land in 1876, after twenty years of the missionary life, and she died here two years later.

These are the four young people who with hearts aflame with love and enthusiasm for Christ and His lost sheep in Syria arrived at Damascus December 13, 1856, to study the language and explore the land for a location for the new mission.

After spending the winter at Damascus in the study of Arabic, and the hot summer months in a mountain village nearby where their study could be continued under more favorable conditions, we find them in the following October (1857) attempting to open work in Zahleh.

ZAHLEH

Zahleh, a large town in the Lebanons about twenty miles east of Beirut, is the headquarters of the Greek Uniate Church of the Lebanons. They are closely affiliated with the Maronites who, like them, acknowledge the Pope of Rome but maintain a separate organization. Three-fifths of the population of the Lebanons is of the Maronite Church.

As our missionaries were able at the time to rent only part of one house, sufficient for only one of the families, it was decided that Mr. Beattie and family should remain in Damascus another winter, but Mr. Dodds moved his family to Zahleh and began to try to give them his Gospel message, though only in a small way, as his ten months' study of Arabic was not enough to prepare him for active work in that difficult language, and it was eight months yet before he preached his first Arabic sermon. He was not by any means idle, however, during the seven months he was allowed to remain in Zahleh, for the Metropolitan or Head of the Greek Uniate Church who regarded Zahleh as his peculiar domain, seemed to feel like a lion being bearded in his den and soon began to make it warm for the unwelcome guest.

Mr. Dodds held on tenaciously and was able to rent an additional house in the spring and Mr. Beattie moved his household goods there before leaving for a visit to the Holy Land in April, 1858. The arrival of these goods in Zahleh so increased the fury of the Metropolitan that he sent his priests to urge Mr. Dodds more effectively to depart, and on his refusing, they threatened to bring a mob and drive him out. He said: "Let the mob come. I will not move." Then they said: "We will begin the work ourselves," and they threw most of his library into the street. Seeing his beloved books being treated thus, Mr. Dodds at last decided that discretion was indicated, and promised to leave the next day, on which the priests had his books restored to their place inside and set some muleteers to work at once packing up all his goods to be ready for the journey. The next morning the priests came again and made sure that he really left the town. To the credit of the Turkish civil authorities we have to record that they refused to assist the Metropolitan in this nefarious business though they were powerless to prevent it when such a high church dignitary was behind it.

Prolonged and vigorous protests and pleas with the aid of the British and American Consuls, while seemingly successful so far as the civil authorities were able to go, did not give grounds of confidence that they could work in Zahleh with any satisfaction. After spending a while in a mountain village, they therefore moved to Beirut for the winter, where they continued to study Arabic and preach some as opportunity offered.

It is good to relate that eighteen years after Mr. Dodds and Mr. Beattie were thus defeated in their plan to settle at Zahleh, Dr. Metheny visited the town and received a fine welcome there by a flourishing Presbyterian Mission, at which one of the members arose and expressed his sorrow that he had been one of the rabble that had cast stones at the caravan of Mr. Dodds as it left their town.

LATAKIA

Before settling down to study in Beirut Mr. Dodds made a trip of exploration to North Syria, visiting Latakia, Antioch and Alexandretta, returning to Beirut October 14, 1858. Largely as a result of this trip they decided to make Latakia the field of their next effort in founding a mission.

So in October, 1859, the two families moved to Latakia by sea and were hospitably entertained for a month at the home of the English Consul until they were able to rent houses for themselves.

Preaching services were begun as soon as they had moved into their own rented rooms, namely, in December, 1859, and have been continued regularly ever since.

A Boys' School was opened at once also with two teachers brought with them from Beirut and one secured in the town. The enrollment reached fifty-five that first year, in spite of the active position of the Greek Church Bishop and his priests.

PROVIDENTIAL GUIDANCE

Subsequent events show the marvelous and merciful providence of God in leading our missionaries out of Zahleh and to the city and province of Latakia. At the very time they were moving to this new location a terrible and cruel war broke out in the Zahleh region between the Maronites and Druzes, largely provoked by the Maronites. Government troops were sent into the region to stop the trouble but as is characteristic of Turkish troops in such cases they really simply joined with the fanatical Druzes, and after officially disarming the Christians, promising to protect them, they helped to slaughter thousands of them. Order was not fully restored until the powers intervened and secured for the Lebanon province a special kind of government under their protection. Then the removal of the Rev. Samuel Lyde just on their arrival and his turning over to them the mission he had founded at Bahamra, left the whole province unoccupied by any other Protestant Mission, while in the Lebanons missions multiplied until there has been keen rivalry among them, especially in the matter of soliciting pupils for their schools.

OUR FIELD

Latakia City and Province is situated in the latitude of North Carolina on the eastern shore of the Mediterranean Sea opposite the Island of Cyprus. The province is about eighty miles north and south by fifty east and west. It is about the size of the state of Connecticut, but its population of 280,000 is about one-fifth that of Connecticut. It is composed of 180,000 Nusairiyeh or Alaweets, 60,000 Moslems and 40,000 Christians of various sects, mostly Creek Catholics or Eastern Orthodox, the eastern division of the Church resulting from the great schism of 1854 when the Bishop of Rome "excommunicated" all the churches of his rival for the highest place in the Church, the Bishopric of Constantinople. A plain of from one to ten miles in width runs the length of the province and gradually merges into the Nusairiyeh range of mountains which rise on the east of the province in some places to four thousand feet above the sea, but descend almost precipitately to the Orontes River on the eastern side.

It has a climate much like that of southern California or northern Florida. But it is cursed with malaria and other diseases, so that the newcomer must be very careful or he will succumb to some of them. Even in the more sanitary homes of the missionaries mosquito nets must be used nearly all the year if malaria is to be avoided.

Until early in this century the only roads in the province were foot paths and the only river crossings were fords.

The city of Latakia is the only town of much importance. It is a corrupt spelling of Laodicea which is the name given to it by its founder in 312 B. C., in honor of his mother, Laodice. It is not to be confused with one of the "Seven Churches of Asia," of that name which was far to the northwest in the region of Smyrna. It has a population of about 25,000 three-fourths of whom are Moslems and the rest nominal Christians. Its houses are built of soft hewn stone, one story in height mostly, and with flat roofs. They are, for the most part, closely crowded together with only donkey paths running between them, except that since the French occupation some streets have been made of normal width. It makes a fine appearance as approached from the sea, the usual way of reaching it until recently. But an American seeing it thus for the first time would never estimate its population at one half of what it really is, nor believe there could be so much ignorance, poverty, filth and misery concealed by such a beautiful exterior.

Much the larger part of the people of the province live in villages on the plain and in the mountains. There the houses are mostly made of mud and rough stones, and poverty and misery reign even more unchallenged than in the city. Most of the villagers are of the Nusairiyeh sect and usually called "Fellaheen" or plowmen, as they are the tillers of the soil for the large land owners. Some of the village people have acquired some land for themselves and work it. They are mostly of the Christian sects, however.

Agriculture is the main employment but it gives very small return for the labor expended, especially since silk culture and tobacco raising have declined almost to the vanishing point.

The vast host of government employees, including soldiers and gendarmes, absorb the cream of the small harvest, leaving very thin skin milk to the tiller of the soil.

The population has changed very little since the time our missionaries came. The birthrate is high but infant mortality is also very high. A mother in one of the better class village homes said she had borne seventeen children of whom only six lived beyond infancy. The number of short graves in the cemeteries is quite impressive even to a casual observer. Emigration has also been a heavy draft on the province all these years.

RELIGIONS OF LATAKIA

(In order of adherents)

THE ALAWEETS (FRENCH ALAOUITES)

The common name is Fellaheen, meaning plowmen, and they were formerly called either Ansyriyeh or Nusairiyeh, being two forms of the plural for the same noun, meaning "Defenders." The religion of these "highlanders" is supposed to be secret and known only to the adult males of the race. Their women, they claim, "are created from the sins of the devil," and have no souls. But a secret shared with so many persons does not long survive. The secrets of this religion were fully exposed in a book published by one of them soon after our work was opened among them. It made a big sensation and caused our missionaries no little anxiety for awhile, as the author seemed disposed to ally himself with them at first after his change of faith but proved to be more eager to be filled with wine than with the Spirit of truth. He was later induced to attend a big Alaweet feast in Adana, made in his honor, they told him. On arrival he was conducted with great ceremony to a central seat on a fine rug which had been carefully spread so as to conceal the open mouth of a well. As soon as he stepped on the rug he dropped into the well and they quickly filled it with stones.

It was known therefore that one of the "distinctive principles" of this religion is that one should play the hypocrite when in the midst of a stronger people of another religion. So we find them out of "respect" to the Moslems, who have so long been their masters, teaching the Koran to their children and using Moslem names as Ali from which comes their name, Alaweets, and Mohammed, the prophet honored by the Moslems. But the initiated among them know that Ali, as they use it, refers not to the Moslem saint of that name but to The Sun, and Mohammed also means to them The Moon. They may be descendants of the old Canaanites and worshippers of Baal. They own respect for the Bible also, but have also their own "Book of Collections" which is mostly a book or ritual and prayers addressed to Ali.

They deem the Milky Way their heaven and each star the departed soul of an Alaweet. One attractive feature of their religion is the sacred preservation of small groves in many spots on their treeless hillsides. In the middle of each of these groves there is a shrine in addition to the numerous ones located in the open. To these shrines a smoking bit of incense is often carried by some child or servant to be offered in behalf of some sick one in the home craving the favor of the god. Sometimes also bloody sacrifices are offered in the groves.

Except for the initiating meetings, the religious "elders" do not seem to do much for their people except to threaten them with dire calamities if they see them inclined to listen to teachers of Christianity. About three-fifths of the people of the Latakia province are of this race, the Alaweets.

It was to them especially that the first efforts of our mission were directed. It was to this people that the door had just been opened in some measure by the Christian zeal and self sacrifice of Rev. Samuel Lyde.

MOSLEMS

So many books have been written on this religion that it seems hardly necessary to say much about it here. What the prophet of Islam might have been had he contacted a robust form of Christianity instead of the paganized emasculated kind he did meet, one can only conjecture. He must be credited with being a more uncompromising foe of idolatry as he found it among the Arabs than the Christians were whom he knew, though he made other compromises to win those rough tribes to allegiance to his religion. But he did win them and seriously threatened for a time to dominate the world with it. And even yet the religion of Mohammed is the greatest challenge to the Church of Christ in all the earth, even since the fall of Turkey as a Moslem power has taken away its head.

A little over one-fifth of the people of our province are Moslems. The influence of our mission among them has been mostly through the school and the Bible women and the distribution of tracts.

THE SECRET SECTS

The Christian Sects, compromising a little less than one-fifth of the population, have this in common which is the special abomination of the Moslems, the worshipping of God by idols in some form. They all use either images or pictures of Jesus and the saints as objects of adoration. All of them hold the virgin Mary and some of the saints in adoration and trust to their intercession. And they all depend largely on their priesthood to work out their salvation for them during their lives, at their death and after death, by reciting of prayers, offering of incense and especially by the offering of "the mass," the sacramental bread "changed" by a priestly formula into "the body of Christ" after being presented to the people to be adored. Much the larger portion of our church members up to the present have come from these sects.

Signs are not wanting that the largest of these, the Greek Orthodox, is slowly disintegrating since its head, the Czar of Russia, has fallen. In Syria an estimated 80,000 of its membership are in open revolt against the Church authorities and propose to set up an independent Church.

The First Decade, 1856-1866

The first three years of this period were spent by our missionaries, Dodds and Beattie, in studying the language and the land. They needed a knowledge of the language to preach and a knowledge of the land to decide where to preach. Both were sufficiently acquired to begin more regular mission work at the beginning of 1860.

As both the officially appointed missionaries were ordained ministers it is not surprising to find them putting preaching the gospel in the first line of their attack on the powers of darkness.

And being Protestant preachers it is also no surprise to find them adding at the very beginning teaching as the second line. For their Commission read: "Preach the Gospel—teaching them."

And being human and remembering the example of their Master it is very natural to find them in a very few months urging the Board to send them a physician to make healing their third line. This line was not actually established however until near the end of the first decade.

Preaching services were held regularly from the time they were actually settled in Latakia, being conducted all through this period in the homes of the missionaries. Besides this regular preaching there was also much informal witnessing to Christ in the villages as they visited them to become more familiar with their field.

For reasons unexplained there was quite a spurt in attendance at the regular city services during 1866 from an average of about 12 to an average of about 50. The arrival of the long expected physician the year previous may have helped the attendance.

The first fruits of their ministry were not slow in appearing. In December, 1860, just a year after beginning in Latakia, they had the great joy of baptizing Hamoud, an Alaweet, of whom Mr. Dodds writes: (at his death four years later) "I never knew one who so steadily and constantly aimed at perfection or so scrupulously shunned every appearance of evil. My companions in the Mission consider this no exaggeration." The death of Mr. Lyde in the previous April must have impressed this, his former pupil, very deeply. He had been under the influence of that godly man at a boy's most impressionable age. He had been a boarder in his school in Bahamra. He had seen him spending and serving unselfishly in trying to alleviate some of the poverty and ignorance about him. Hamoud had doubtless helped to feed the hungry multitudes who came twice a week to be fed by Mr. Lyde's bounty.

Then he had heard of the dastardly trick played upon his beloved teacher by Alaweets of a distant village. Luring him into their midst by a pretense of wishing to learn about his religion, one hundred and fifty of them had cursed him and beaten him and declared they were going to kill him then and there. Then Hamoud would see him being brought home almost dead, and then taken to Latakia for medical aid, and at last leaving for Alexandria, Egypt, where he lingered but a few months until he died. Yet he forbade his friends to seek any vengeance on his persecutors. Mr. Dodds credits Hamoud's conversion largely to such influences used by the Holy Spirit.

A second Alaweet, Yusuf Jadeed, another of Mr. Lyde's pupils, was baptized in 1864, and his life was a credit to all his Christian teachers, for he remained faithful under severe persecution.

The third convert, Maryam, baptized in 1865, is an even more remarkable evidence of the work of the Spirit. An Alaweet woman brought up in the belief that women had no souls and religion was not for them, she had even further to come out of the darkness of paganism than either Hamoud or Yusuf. But in her Christian life and at her death in 1871 she gave abundant evidence that her conversion was real.

At the end of this first decade seven had been admitted to the communion of our Church in Syria.

SCHOOLS WERE OPENED

The Boys' School opened early in 1860 and was continued through the decade with an attendance of about sixty. An average of ten Alaweet boys were under the special care of the missionaries during this time as boarders. Mr. Lyde had arranged, in dying, to have a sum of $300 annually paid to our Mission from his estate for the Alaweet work. This was paid regularly until 1869.

The Girls' School, although asked for early in the period, was not opened until 1865 when forty girls came under the instruction of a teacher brought from Beirut.

Village Schools also were not opened until 1865, when four villages among the Alaweets were furnished teachers, and a total of fifty-seven boys began to learn the first principles of Gospel truth.

MEDICAL WORK

The Medical Department was really opened in a way soon after the arrival of Dr. Metheny in 1865, but he could not give his whole time to it until after some time spent in the study of the language.

Dr. David Metheny was added to the original group of missionaries during this decade but he did not arrive until near the end of it, in December, 1864. He served with great zeal and skill in Latakia until 1883 when he responded to a call from Cilicia and opened the Tarsus Mission where he served until his death in June, 1897. When home on furlough in 1873 he was ordained to preach also, so from that time he did valiant service both as a preacher and doctor.

Although a most kind and gentle Christian gentleman Dr. Metheny was in an emphatic sense a soldier of Christ. He was an almost invincible fighter in the cause of the oppressed against the tyranny of the ruling overlords. Some of his experiences in this line were quite dramatic. On one occasion the Governor ordered troops to go to the Mission in Mersine and remove an Alaweet boy whom Dr. Metheny had repeatedly refused to surrender. A telegram had been sent inviting a United States warship to visit the Mission. The morning of the crisis the doctor had all the outside doors barricaded and an armed guard at each door on the inside. Members of the family were anxiously scanning the sea for a sign of the coming warship. Just as the first sound of the bugles of the Turkish troops fell on their ears they discerned the first smoke of the approaching ship rising above the horizon and with glad relief passed the news to the doctor, who at once dispatched a diplomatic message to the Governor telling him a United States Captain was just coming into harbor and would be wanting to pay his respects to the Governor and it was hoped arrangements could be made to receive him. The troops were at once turned back to their barracks. The Alaweet boy remained in school.

At Dr. Metheny's death after thirty-three years of service in the Mission he was buried in the Mission garden, there being no Protestant cemetery there then. Complaint was made to this same Governor about it. He exclaimed: "What! Is the American doctor dead? Is he really buried?" On being assured that he was really under ground the Governor gave a sigh of relief and a wave of the hand, dismissing the informer with the remark: "Let him lie. Don't disturb him."

Mrs. Emma Gregg Metheny, wife of the above, came with him to the field and served with him until her death in 1876, twelve years in all. Though much of the time in delicate health, her life was a living witness to the power of Christ. She contributed liberally to the maintenance of the Mission.

In the Board's report to Synod in 1866 at the end of this period we read: "It is now ten years since the organization of the Mission, and the interest in it manifested by other people continues unabated. We are able to say what perhaps no other Church in the country can say in regard to its foreign work, no year has closed with an indebted or even exhausted treasury." This is the more remarkable when we recall that in the later years of this decade our country went through that terrific struggle to save the Union.

GIRLS' SCHOOL BUILDING, LATAKIA, SYRIA

View as seen from Fattal's house. This street is called American Street Steps in right of picture go up to house of Toufeek Awad, the brother of the Pastor, his house being the lower story. Miss Edgar's house is in the middle of the picture.

The Second Decade, 1866-1876

NEW BUILDINGS

This was the *building period* of the mission. During these ten years the three story building which now houses the Girls' School was erected at a cost of $7,000. It was originally built to house both day and boarding schools for both boys and girls, and was so used for some years. The first two stories were divided by a stone wall running clear through the building, on one side of which the boys slept, ate and went to school; and on the other side the girls.

The third story was arranged to provide a home for the missionaries who were in charge of the schools. The site was purchased and the work of construction begun in 1867. Three story buildings were then quite rare in Latakia and are yet, for that matter. But it has stood the test of time very well, having passed through several earthquake shocks, one of them in April, 1872, being severe enough to drive many out of the city and to force the missionaries to resort to tents. The city of Antioch, only seventy miles north was nearly destroyed at the time.

The hospital building was erected for a double missionary residence in 1875 and was first occupied by the Metheny and Easson families. Only $1,250.00 cash was furnished for it by the Board, the missionaries then on the ground providing the balance in various ways, as by personal contributions, medical fees and payment of rent in advance. It has experienced many alterations and would hardly be recognizable to the original builders. Adapting it to use as a hospital and clinic, according to the ideas of the various physicians in charge of it, accounted for most of these changes.

The chapel was built in 1876. It is in a way a monument to Mrs. Emma Gregg Metheny who furnished all the funds for its construction and passed away at the end of this decade just shortly before the building was finished. It served as a house of worship for the Latakia congregation for fifty years until the present church building was erected. It also serves as chapel for the girls' school and the church Sabbath School.

SUADEA REBUILT

After the severe earthquake of 1872, Rev. Henry Easson found the buildings at Suadea so badly damaged that he had to make extensive repairs there. This station was opened by a Dr. Holt-Yates of England some years previous to his death ,which occurred in 1873. His widow then persuaded our Mission to take over the property, promising to contribute about $1,500.00 a year on condition that a school and general mission work would be carried on there. Mr. Easson and his wife arrived in Latakia just at this time, so the very next year (1874) they were sent to Suadea and spent a year there getting it in shape to continue the work as stipulated.

BAHAMRA REPAIRED

The property left us by Rev. Mr. Lyde at this place in 1860 had been little used except for a day school until in 1870, the plan to have both boys' and girls' boarding schools in the one building at Latakia having proved unsatisfactory after a three years trial, it was decided to move the boys' boarding school to Bahamra, which necessitated extensive repairs there also. The boys' boarding school remained there until the end of this decade, 1876, when it was moved back to Latakia. The annual contribution arranged for by Mr. Lyde in his will was discontinued at the death of his brother in 1869. In 1874 Turkish soldiers forced an entrance into the Bahamra school and carried off five of our Alaweet converts to prison. They made their escape however, after a few months in prison, and returned to their village. This interrupted school work there for awhile.

THE GIRLS' SCHOOL

Under the rule of the Turk no one felt secure unless the lot on which his home was built was surrounded by a stone wall high enough to prevent people looking in or coming in without much difficulty except through the strong door made in the wall for that purpose. So when the garden was bought on which to make the buildings for the Mission mentioned above, it was found the wall must be rebuilt also, necessitating quite an outlay of money.

VILLAGE BUILDINGS

Two two-room buildings were made during this period in two separate villages where no room suitable could be found to house either the teacher or the school.

ALEPPO-IDLIB

In 1867 the Free Church of Scotland withdrew from Aleppo and Idlib and turned the mission work there over to us. Dr. Dodds, who with his family returned from their first furlough this year, was appointed by the Board to take charge of the Aleppo station. There were about one hundred and twenty pupils under instruction at the two places. At the death of Dr. Dodds in 1870 the work was abandoned until the Idlib part of it was reopened by Rev. James Martin of the Scotch-Irish Covenanter Church. He came to Latakia and assisted some in the medical work there while studying the language, arriving in 1872 and going to Antioch to open work in 1876. From Antioch he supervised the work at Idlib until his retirement in 1924. Since then it has been under the direction of Dr. S. H. Kennedy of Alexandretta of the same Church. A flourishing school and congregation are being carried on with Syrian workers.

NEW RECRUITS

This decade brought a goodly number of new missionaries to reinforce the little band at Latakia. Of these the first was Miss Rebecca Crawford who arrived in 1867 to help in taking care of the girls' school. She remained twelve years in our Mission, but in 1879 was carried off by Dr. Martin of the Antioch Mission to "be a helpmeet for him."

The second arrival was in 1872 when Rev. S. R.

Galbraith and wife came out and entered with great promise into the study of the language, but in less than a year he was called to higher service and the sorrow stricken young bride returned to the States.

Miss Mary Ellen Dodds, daughter of the pioneer, Dr. R. J. Dodds, one of the two children he had left behind with relatives when he first came to Syria, followed him to his chosen field in 1872. After five years in the field in language study and school work she was married to Dr. David Metheny and served with him at Latakia and Mersine and Tarsus until his death in 1897, a total of twenty-five years.

Rev. James Martin and wife from the Irish Church arrived at Latakia in 1872 and remained until the end of the decade in 1876, when he moved to Antioch where he labored under direction of the Scotch-Irish Board until 1924, when he returned to Ireland, a total of fifty-two years. Although trained as a physician as well as a preacher, he soon decided to confine himself to preaching as the more important work of the missionary of the cross. He was an untiring worker and had an excellent knowledge of the Arabic. He was on furlough during the war years.

Again in 1873 the Mission was strengthened by the arrival of Rev. Henry Easson and wife. They labored in Latakia until 1892 when, after four years in the home land they accepted work in Cyprus and served there until 1901. He has left a reputation for great physical strength among the Syrians. A sample story is that on one occasion when he could not get the animal he was riding to cross a shallow stream, he got off and threw his arms around it and carried it across. They do not tell the weight of the animal, but if it was strong enough to carry Mr. Easson it must have been a good weight for a man to carry. The act made a sensation anyway.

The last of the reinforcements to arrive in this decade was Miss Mattie R. Wylie who came in 1875 and served until her death in 1916, a total of over forty years. Her last years were full of suffering, but by her Christian patience and hope she preached as effectively during those years as when she was stronger in body.

PROMOTIONS

The first adult death in our Mission was that of Dr. R. J. Dodds, who died of Typhus fever after a short illness at Aleppo in 1870, leaving his wife and five boys and two girls to make their sorrowful way to the home land. But He who has promised to be "the husband of the widow and the father of the fatherless" was faithful to his promise, and three of the sons grew up to follow in the footsteps of their honored father and labor as missionaries in the same Mission. The rest of the family made a good record also.

The second death was that of Rev. Mr. Galbraith in 1872 which has been noted. Then followed in 1876 the death of Mrs. Emma Gregg Metheny and that of Mrs. James Martin. Dr. Martin also suffered the loss of an infant child this same year and the Eassons also were bereaved this year of an infant daughter.

During this second decade preaching was carried on regularly in Latakia city and in three of the villages. Attendance increased greatly until a climax was reached in the last communion of the period, delayed a little for the completion of the new chapel: it was held in March, 1877, when four hundred attended. The total accessions reached ninety-seven, a good part of them Alaweets. One of these last was Maryam, the first female convert from that pagan sect. Another was Mahmoud, the first adult to join us from that sect, after being fully initiated into that religion. His daughter had been brought in through the schools, and kept praying earnestly for the conversion of her father with the result recorded.

School work was prosecuted with increasing vigor and interest. Early in the decade a rebellion of the Alaweets necessitated the closing of the village schools among them for two years, but they were reopened later. The boarding pupils, boys and girls, reached as high as one hundred and fifty-two, of which one hundred and seven were girls and forty-five boys. Seven village schools had a total of one hundred and fifty-five additional male pupils.

Medical work begun at the first of this decade was carried on by Dr. David Metheny with good success the whole of the ten years, the average cash receipts being $500 annually.

It is interesting to record that although the panic year 1873 occurred in this period when Iowa corn was sold by the writer's father for eleven cents for two bushel of ears and so many chose to use their corn for fuel instead of wood, our Foreign Board was nevertheless able to report a balance each year of from $3,000 to $5,000. And expenditures were extra large, due to so much building and the sending out of six new missionaries and the returning of six on furlough or retirement and the raising of a special fund of several thousand for widow Dodds and children. This fine record was made also without the aid of a Synod budget plan and with no endowment income. "There were giants in those days."

Front view of the Girls' School building. At left through foliage, the corner of the church is seen.

The Third Decade, 1876-1886

This period opened with war clouds looming black on the horizon in the Near East, which burst in the thunder and storm of conflict between Russia and Turkey in the spring of 1877. The war was of short duration and resulted in the complete defeat of Turkey before the end of that year. The Treaty of San Stefano between the two powers is described as "the dictation of relentless power to a crushed and helpless state." The "powers" however appeared at "the killing," represented by the British fleet, and prevented the final blow being struck, the capture of Constantinople, thus securing another reprieve for "The Sick Man of the East." Enough was retained in the Treaty of Berlin, which was forced on Russia as a substitute for the San Stefano Treaty, to improve greatly the conditions of the Christian minorities under the Turk—if and when the reforms promised, even in the Berlin Treaty, were carried out faithfully by the Sultan.

But the sequel demonstrated again what had been repeatedly made clear before in the dealings of the powers with the Turkish government namely, "That many cooks spoil the broth." The rule of the Turk, as he saw it, was the rule of true believers over infidels, when non-Moslems were concerned, and he conceded to "infidels" (Christians) no rights except the right to live on the payment of tribute, and that only as long as it suited the Sultan's convenience to have them live.

When street dogs so multiplied in Constantinople that even the Sultan was convinced they must be removed, his tender Moslem conscience would not permit him to give an order for their death, but he decreed that they should be exiled to a barren island in the bay where, he said, "if they die it will be an act of Allah." But that tenderness of conscience about taking life did not seem to function when he wished to free any place in his realm from Armenians.

Again and again, Armenian Christians were massacred by the thousands after he had given his solemn promise to "protect" them. And the epithet applied to them in the very act of killing them was "Christian Dogs."

Two weddings in the field changed the personnel of the Mission early in this third period. Dr. Metheny in December, 1877, married Miss Mary Ellen Dodds, teacher in the girls' school. They went to the United States the following spring on furlough and remained until June, 1879.

Dr. James Martin married Miss Rebecca Crawford in 1879 and took her also out of the girls' school to his station at Antioch.

Miss Mattie R. Wylie was thus left alone in charge of that school and continued on duty there the whole of this decade, except for a short furlough when she had to accompany Miss Carson home, as she was compelled to resign in the Fall of 1880 on account of ill health.

Rev. Henry Easson and wife went on furlough in 1882 and returned to the field in 1883. They spent three years with the boys' boarding school in Suadea just before going on this furlough. This boarding school was then brought to Latakia again and housed in the lower part of what was later the hospital building, but had been used up to that time as a residence for missionaries.

Dr. Joseph Beattie and wife were at home on furlough at the beginning of the period and he was chosen Moderator of the Synod of 1877. He returned to Latakia alone in 1878, but after only a few months was called back to the States by the death of his wife who had been left at home to attend to the education of the children. He did not take up work in the Mission again until 1881, when he returned for the special purpose of teaching a class in theology to prepare a native ministry. He was spared to this special task only two years when, in October, 1883, he was called to join his wife in the higher service of heaven. He received the degree of D. D. while home in 1878.

The unplanned and unexpected departure of Dr. Beattie on the report of his wife's death left the two young ladies, Miss Wylie and Miss Crawford as the only missionaries at Latakia for a while. During that time the Moslems of the baser sort seized the opportunity to show their contempt for women by making threatening demonstrations against the school and the pupils. Things were beginning to look rather serious for our lonely young missionaries when, providentially and most opportunely, a U. S. man-of-war appeared on the horizon headed for Latakia. As soon as it anchored in the roadstead, the captain came ashore and after calling on the missionaries he paid his respects to the Latakia governor. During the official call he found opportunity to tell the governor impressively that the U. S. government expected the Turkish government of Latakia to furnish full protection to these two American women and if the governor was not able to do so, he was there with his man-of-war to assist him in the matter.

A second warship calling a little later added to the deep impression made by the first one, so the attitude of the people was completely changed. Many believed these two ships had come the seven thousand miles from "New York" just to look after these two young ladies of the mission and exclaimed: "Mashallah" (What hath God wrought!)

About the same time the Alaweets of the mountains who were almost in rebellion against the Turks, sent word to Latakia that the Americans of the mission were their particular friends and any injury done to them would be considered sufficient cause for an expedition in force from the mountains to avenge the wrong. Thus the wrath of men was made to praise the Lord and the remainder of wrath was restrained.

NEW RECRUITS

Rev. W. J. Sproull and wife and Miss Mary E.

Carson came out in 1879 with Dr. Metheny and family, who were returning then from furlough. Mr. and Mrs. Sproull remained only to the end of the decade, a period of seven years. He showed great ability in mastering the difficult language and rendering valuable service. No reason is given in the records for his resignation, which was accepted by both the missionaries and the Board with expressions of deep regret and the highest esteem and appreciation. After a pastorate of five years in the home Church he united with the Presbyterian Church.

Miss Carson was able to remain only a year when her health failed and so she had to return home.

Dr. Archibald Dodds, son of the pioneer, born in Damascus the next spring after the coming of our missionaries to Syria, arrived in Latakia in November, 1881, along with Miss Evadna Sterrett.

Dr. Dodds was married the year after his arrival to Miss Mizpah Metheny, daughter of Dr. David Metheny, but after only two years and a half of service together the young wife was called to the eternal home, leaving to his sole care their infant child. When returning from a trip home, to put this child in the care of his mother, the ship in which he travelled was shipwrecked off Gibraltar and he was drowned. His stateroom companion, who survived along with nearly all the other passengers and crew, reported that he had made desperate efforts to save Dr. Dodds but failed, as, he said, Dr. Dodds could not swim and had no life belt, having given the two he was able to procure to women whom he found without one. Thus was "nipped in the bud" a very promising career, but if the Master wished to pluck the "bud" who shall complain?

Miss Evadna Sterrett, who came out with Dr. Dodds in 1881, had a fine long term of service in the field, most of it at Mersine. She conducted a school there alone the first two years, with Dr. Metheny laboring at Tarsus, eighteen miles away. She was married to Dr. Balph in the autumn of 1919 and served with him at Latakia until his resignation in 1926, thus completing about forty-five years of missionary work.

She was a most faithful, efficient and sympathetic worker, always sharing in quiet but material ways the burdens of the many poor who came to her notice.

Another arrival in the year 1881 which gave much joy to the missionaries and their Syrian brethren in the Church, was that of Daoud Suleiman. He with some other Alaweet converts had been carried off eight years before and impressed into the Turkish army on the ground that they were Alaweets and obligated to serve in the army. Yet the government had recognized them as Christians and collected the army exemption tax imposed only on Christians, for several years previous to their arrest. Daoud remained true to the Church all the eight years of hard army life, in spite of many definite and desperate efforts to make him recant. He had been unable to communicate with his friends all that time so he seemed as one risen from the dead when he again appeared among them.

In this connection let us record also a serious loss the missionaries sustained a few years before this in the impressive death of the first woman convert from the Alaweets, Maryam, wife of Yusuf Jadeed. After being ill for some time in the village where her husband was teaching, and attended as best they could by the missionaries, Dr. Metheny and Mr. Beattie, she begged very much to be brought to Latakia to escape the petty persecutions of her Alaweet neighbors who have little sympathy for one who is sick for a long time. So it was arranged to have her carried on a stretcher by porters the eight hour journey to the city, where she was welcomed by her Christian friends. But she rapidly grew worse and after repeating in a clear voice the Twenty-third Psalm and commending her two little children to the care of her friends she exclaimed: "The Lord be glorified," and fell asleep in the Lord. Thus entered into rest the first fruits from Alaweet women, so far as is known. Her consistent life and faithful confession of her Christian faith and the calm confidence of her death made a deep impression on many.

Our mission field was further enlarged this decade by the opening of the Tarsus Mission, with headquarters first at Tarsus, the birthplace of the great apostle to the Gentiles, but later at Mersine. Work was conduced at Adana, Tarsus, and Mersine, all good sized towns, and also at some villages. On the arrival of Mr. Doods in 1881, making two physicians at Latakia, the mission and the Board acquiesced in the strong desire of Dr. Metheny to carry the gospel to the many Alaweet immigrants on the plains of Cilicia or Asia Minor. So, on Dr. Metheny's return from furlough in 1882, he and his family and Miss Evadna Sterrett moved to that region. Miss Sterrett opened a school at Mersine and Dr. Metheny opened work in Tarsus, but later moved also to Mersine and, at his own expense, put up capacious buildings for residences and for boys' and girls' day and boarding schools.

Boarding schools were opened in 1885 and for ten years were kept going all the year round, being moved to Guzne in the Taurus mountains in the hot months. Here also the doctor bought land and erected buildings both for the missionaries and for the two schools with his own money. After ten years the boarders were sent home in summer.

On one of his many trips from Guzne to Mersine a couple of bandits attempted to hold up the doctor but his sharp eye discovered them waiting for him and he got the drop on them and marched them ahead of him to the city where he gave them into custody.

In 1883 a metrical version of the Psalms in Arabic was published in co-operation with the U. P. Mission of Egypt. It is the one still used by both our people and those of the Scotch-Irish Mission north of us, although there is strong demand for a better one.

The schools continued to grow in number and attendance until we had twenty-seven schools going with 828 pupils. A goodly number of these were boarders, mostly Alaweets, who were taught, fed and clothed free of charge, generally. The popularity of this branch of the work was evidenced by special contributions at home for the opening of new schools in the villages. One society sent enough to support four village teachers, one year.

Evangelism in the direct form was pushed with vigor during the decade by the preachers, Easson, Sproull, and Metheny, the latter being ordained when home on furlough in 1873. One of Mr. Beattie's pupils was licensed also in 1882 and was an effective evangelist.

The number of communicants more than doubled in the ten years, reaching 186 without counting the missionaries.

Medical work prospered also under Dr. Metheny and Dr. Dodds. The fees collected reached as high as $600 a year and averaged $485, although most of the service was rendered free, due to the extreme poverty of most of the applicants.

Efforts of the Syrian converts to share in the work resulted early in this period in the forming of a Missionary Society of the Syrians, both men and women. Subscriptions made at the first meeting totaled $16 a month, when dollars were "as good as gold."

An important event occurred at home during this decade when Dr. S. O. Wylie, who had fathered the work of foreign missions in our Church from the beginning in 1856, was translated to the Church above and seems to have dropped his mantle in this respect on Dr. R. M. Sommerville whose signature is attached to most of the annual reports to Synod from that time until his death.

The Board again reported handsome balances in all its annual financial reports during this third decade.

MISSION GROUNDS, LATAKIA, SYRIA

Foreground, girls' school building S. W. view. Building in background with three chimneys is the boys' school building. Other tile roofs in left of pic ure are the roof of the hospital building.

The Fourth Decade, 1886-1896

The thirtieth anniversary of the founding of the Syrian Mission found nine missionaries on the ground, of the twenty-two who had come to the field in the thirty years and had averaged ten years of service each. Eight of these died "in the harness"; two went home on the death of their husbands in the field; two resigned for reasons not recorded; one was invalided home. Of the nine who remained on duty, Rev. and Mrs. Henry Easson continued to labor at Latakia and in the out-stations, including Suadea which was a hard two-days horse-back ride over the mountains to the north, and Tartoos, a two-days ride also to the south. His health at last failed and he and his wife went home in 1892. But after four years they accepted appointment again from the Board to the new field of Cyprus in the last year of this decade, 1896.

Miss Mattie R. Wylie served all of this fourth period in the school for girls at Latakia, except the year of her furlough, 1889.

Dr. Jas. Martin and his American wife carried on the work in Antioch under the direction of the Scotch-Irish Church whose work is to be included to give a view of all the Covenanter work in Syria. Mrs. Rebecca Crawford Martin, his wife, ended her term of service on earth with the end of this decade in 1896, making a total of thirty years for her in the field.

Miss Meta Cunningham, who came out from Ireland in 1883, labored at Suadea, although supported by the Scotch-Irish Board until 1895 when by general agreement of all concerend she was transferred to our Board. She was a most energetic and zealous missionary, giving a fine ministry of both healing and teaching to the poor of the Suadea valley.

Dr. David Metheny and wife spent this ten years in preaching and healing at Mersine Mission, except for a furlough in 1889.

Miss Evadna M. Sterrett was the efficient head of the schools at Mersine all of the period except for a furlough in 1889.

NEW ARRIVALS

The Fourth Decade was the richest of all the eight in volunteers for the Foreign Field. The Student Volunteer Movement was launched at the opening of the period in 1886 in a conference at Northfield, and may have had some influence in the zeal of its first years in attracting the young people of our Church to this glorious service. We only know that no less than twenty-eight young people from our little Church accepted service in the Foreign Mission field during this ten years, almost one and a half times as many as had come out in the *thirty* years previous. Four of this consecrated group were sent to the new field in Cyprus, opened in 1891. Four opened our foreign work in China in 1895 and twenty came to Syria, one of them from Ireland.

Of the twenty Miss Maggie B. Edgar came first in November, 1886. She taught some English in the boys' school even while learning the Arabic and then aided Miss Wylie in the girls' school or had charge of one or other of the schools at Latakia for many years. The last few years she labored as Bible woman, until her sudden disappearance on January 25, 1932, completing the longest term of service of any of the missionaries who came from America, a little more than forty-five years.

The second of the twenty to reach the field was Miss Lillian Joseph of Hopkinton, Ia., who came to Mersine in May, 1887, and assisted Miss Sterrett in the schools there until persistent illness compelled her to return home in 1892, after only five years in the work.

The third was Miss Willia Dodds of Beaver Falls, who came with Miss Joseph to help Dr. Metheny in his medical work, but a few months later, in November, 1887, she was appointed to Latakia to assist in the girls' school while Miss Wylie went on furlough. In 1889 we find her back at Mersine to help Miss Joseph while Miss Sterrett was on furlough. She was again summoned to Latakia by the last illness of her sister, Mrs. Balph, and after her sister's death she took Dr. Balph's children to the home land, and got back to Mersine in November, 1893, and helped in the schools until the next year she was again brought to Latakia to help in the girls' school while Miss Edgar went on furlough. She continued to serve at Latakia in one capacity and another until a stroke of paralysis, in February, 1904, compelled her to retire, after seventeen years of mission labor.

Dr. Jas. M. Balph of Rose Point, Pa., was the fourth of the score of new recruits and he reached Latakia in October, 1887, and took over the medical work left by Dr. Dodds when he was drowned in October, 1885. He had a long term of most acceptable service in tri-weekly clinics and hospital and house visits until he resigned in 1926, a total of thirty-nine years of service. His wife, Mrs. Elzina Dodds Balph, and their three children came with him, but she was on the field only five years when she was called away to serve at the court of the King, leaving a new born daughter and her other children to the care of her bereaved husband and sisters.

Rev. Jas. S. Stewart came to Latakia in the fall of 1888 and was associated with Rev. Henry Easson only four years when the latter's resignation left him the only minister in that part of Syria. He was in active service in the Mission until his retirement in 1920, thirty-two years. On his second furlough in 1910 he was chosen moderator of Synod and also was honored with the degree of D.D. by Geneva College. For twenty years he was not only missionary pastor but head of the boys' school in Latakia also. His wife, Mrs. Mary Scott Stewart, and their two children came with him. She was an active helper in the home and in the church through all the thirty-two years of their joint sojourn in Syria. Both of them came from Pittsburgh Presbytery.

Rev. R. J. Dodds, son of the pioneer, born in Latakia, was the third of his father's children to follow the father's footsteps to the Syrian field, and the eighth to arrive in this fourth decade. He came to Mersine in

November, 1890. After only five years on the field he felt it necessary to resign in 1895, but after the death of Dr. David Metheny (his brother-in-law) in 1897, he again accepted appointment to that field and labored there for ten years more, making fifteen years in all. Having acquired the Arabic as a child he was the more efficient in presenting the message to the people. His wife, Mrs. Jennie Garret Dodds, came out with him and gave him efficient help. Their union was blessed with nine fine children who today treasure their memories.

Mrs. Mary McCracken McCarroll, the tenth on the list, reached Latakia in November, 1890, and was associated with Miss Edgar in the work of the girls' school. But after only a year and a half in our work she was married to Rev. J. S. Crawford of Damascus, another Irishman who found a wife in the Latakia Mission circle.

Rev. J. Boggs Dodds left a pleasant pastorate of only nine months duration, at Olathe, Kansas, to obey the urge, incited by the plea of Miss Meta Cunningham of Suadea, to preach the gospel to the people of Syria. He arrived in February, 1893, and labored at Suadea with great energy until sickness in his family caused him to resign, soon after their return from his first furlough in 1903. But such was his devotion to the people of Suadea that he again left a loyal congregation at home and came out alone in 1906 to carry on until a new missionary could acquire enough of the language to take over the work there. This time he remained two years, making his total service in the field twelve years. His wife, Mrs. Myrta May Dodds, came out with him and was his active and efficient helper until her health and that of one of their four boys caused their return. Her total time in the field was ten years. These were the first to come to Syria from Kansas Presbytery, which later sent so many to the field.

Miss Jennie B. Dodds, sister of Rev. J. B., came in November, 1893, and in a very short time was reported to be "serving like a veteran" in the school work at

Mersine. But in visting her brother in vacations she came under the eyes of a young Irishman (Mr. Kennedy) who had recently come out to Antioch unattached, and the result was a wedding in 1897, a vacancy in the working force of Mersine and a decided reinforcement for the mission at Antioch.

Dr. W. M. Moore also came to Suadea in November, 1893, to open medical work there. He ministered to the needy of that valley successfully until the end of this decade in 1896, when he was transferred by the Board to the new field in Cyprus. His wife, Mrs. Kate McNaughton Moore, accompanied him and took her full part in the work that fell to them to do in Syria and later in Cyprus.

Miss Lizzie McNaughton, sister of Mrs. Moore, came out with them and was stationed at Latakia to help in the schools there. She was transferred to Mersine and labored in school work there faithfully until 1903, a total of ten years in the field.

Rev. Samuel H. Kennedy came out to the field from the R. P. Church in Ireland in December, 1895, and was for a time with Dr. Martin in the work of that church in Antioch. In November, 1902, he and his wife opened the fine work at the port of Alexandretta which they have carried on with great energy and success until the present.

Dr. S.A. S. Metheny returned to the scenes of his childhood and took up the work left vacant by his noble father the year following his arrival in August, 1896. But after only four years in the field he found it necessary to resign for health reasons and return to the States. His wife, Mrs. Margaret Slater Metheny, came with him. It was with the deep regret of the Board and the Mission they were released from the work.

The last of this score of new arrivals in this fourth decade was Mrs. Penelope Allen Balph, who was persuaded by Dr. Balph to accompany him as his helpmate on his return from furlough in 1896. She served actively and faithfully in Latakia until their furlough in 1913 from which she was not allowed to return, as she was called to the heavenly service in 1917 before the armistice opened the way for their return to Latakia. She had eighteen years in the field.

Some of the strong attractions to Syria which operated so effectively on these twenty young people seem also to have been active in some of the members of the Board and other friends of the Mission, for in 1888 we find a "delegation" composed of Dr. David McAllister and elder Henry O'Neil, and others not official, toiling over the Alaweet hills on horseback to visit the several villages where schools were in operation, and sleeping—if they could sleep—with aching back and muscles, in the best the village could afford, and making an unwelcome acquaintance with the voracious flea, and then inspecting the larger work in the city. Again two days of still more wearying horseback climbing over the mountains north to Kessab on a trail only the most sure footed animals could negotiate, and down again on the other side to Suadea to look over the schools there and incidentally to get a look at the old stone pier where Paul set sail on the First Foreign Mission. A half day ride took them to Antioch where the self-effacing Barnabas introduced Paul to the work in real earnest, and then on by horse and boat to the port of Mersine and on horse again to Tarsus where humble followers of the great Apostle of the Gentiles, representing the Covenanters, were visited and encouraged in their work of building a spiritual monument to mark his birth place. One more journey over the great plain took them to Adana, the capital of the province where another group of our mission were found spreading the good tidings of salvation among the poor of that city and its environs.

The next year Dr. D. B. Wilson and his sister followed this first party on a tour of our field. And in 1890 Dr. J. W. Sproull gave the mission a visit. And in the spring of 1896 the corresponding secretary of the Board, Dr. R. M. Sommerville, came with his wife to see for himself something of the work he was giving so much of his mighty energy to keep going.

In another way this was more literally a golden age of the mission. An endowment had been accumulating slowly during previous decades but in 1892, by the handsome gift of elder David Gregg of Pittsburgh, father of Mrs. David (Gregg) Metheny who died at Latakia, and other bequests, this fund was trebled, reaching $100,000. This consecrated money has furnished an income ever since, sufficient to maintain six or seven of our missionaries in the field.

There is a dark background however to throw into stronger relief these brighter features. The Turkish authorities were increasingly hostile and active, especially to the school work. But the descendants of the Covenanters, who defied a hostile government in Scotland to obey God, were only stiffened in their determination by such opposition and the work went on. Many hundreds of children were taught the imperishable truths of the Word so they could never forget them, and many souls were brought into the glorious light and liberty of the Gospel. The total accessions were more than doubled again in the ten years, reaching 479 in all, not counting those at Antioch.

An average of six or seven thousand patients were treated at the three stations and their environs, Latakia, Suadea, and Mersine, the remedy for the body being always accompanied by "the balm of Gilead" for the immortal spirit.

The fine $11,000 boys' school building was added to the equipment at Latakia in 1893 under Dr. Stewart's direction.

Brutal massacres of Christian Armenians in Asia Minor struck terror into the hearts of all Christians in Turkey at the close of this fourth decade.

COVENANTER CHURCH, LATAKIA, SYRIA

Dr. Balph Memorial drinking fountain in the foreground, right lower corner.

The Fifth Decade, 1896-1906

At the threshold of the last half of our eight decades we find twenty-one missionaries in the Syrian Mission, including the Scotch-Irish but excluding Cyprus. Six of these remained from the nine we found on the field at the beginning of the fourth decade. Fifteen of the twenty new arrivals in the last decade also remained to begin this new period of service. The eight missing are accounted for briefly as follows:

Rev. H. Easson and wife were invalided home in 1893.

Miss Rebecca (Crawford) Martin died in 1896.

Mrs. Mary (McCracken) McCarroll was removed by marriage in 1892.

Miss Lilian Joseph was invalided home in 1893.

Mrs. Elzina (Dodds) Balph died in 1892.

Dr. and Mrs. Wm. Moore were transferred to Cyprus in 1896.

The twenty-one remaining were located as follows: The Misses Mattie Wylie and Maggie Edgar were conducting the flourishing Girls' Boarding and Day School at Latakia. Rev. J. S. Stewart and wife conducted the Boys' Boarding and Day School there and he also was superintendent of the village schools and pastor-at-large of all the churches in the Latakia province. Dr. Balph and wife with Miss Willa Dodds were in charge of the medical work at Latakia, comprising hospital, clinics, and house visits with occasional trips to the villages to relieve distress.

Miss Lizzie McNaughton was assisting also in the Latakia Girls' School but in 1897, the first year of this decade, she was transferred to Mersine. She was associated there in school work with Miss Evadna Sterrett. Mr. David Metheny and wife began the period in the usual work of preaching and healing but in a very enfeebled condition. His son, Dr. S. A. S. Metheny, and wife were his proficient assistants there in the medical work. Rev. R. J. Dodds was pastor-at-large and superintendent of schools in the same mission.

Miss Jennie Dodds began the period also in the Mersine schools but at the very beginning was transferred by marriage to assist in the work at Antioch as the wife of Rev. S. H. Kennedy, who with Dr. Jas. Martin, recently left a widower for the second time, carried on the work in that mission.

Miss Meta Cunningham was still working energetically to help the people of the Suadea valley both in the schools and in simple medical work. Rev. J. B. Dodds and wife had charge of the preaching and pastoral work there.

NEW ARRIVALS. The first were Rev. C. A. Dodds and wife, Mrs. Annabelle (Campbell) Dodds, who arrived in 1898 at Latakia. He was the fourth child of the pioneer, Rev. R. J. Dodds, to follow up the father's work in Syria. Towards the last of the decade came Rev. A. J. McFarland and wife, Mrs. Isabel (Edgar) McFarland), after a pleasant pastorate of ten years in Kansas City, Mo. With them came Miss Zada Patton, also from Kansas Presbytery (Sterling congregation). The three all reached Latakia in November, 1906, just a month before the jubilee anniversary of the landing of our first missionaries in Syria, December, 1856.

Antioch was reinforced early in the period by the coming of the Linehart sisters of Switzerland, one of them to be the wife of Dr. James Martin and the other to help in the school work. A notable and very welcome arrival was Miss Evangeline Methany also who came to the new station opened at Alexandretta, the port of Antioch, which had been carried on only two years when she arrived in 1904. She was a granddaughter of the pioneer Rev. R. J. Dodds and a daughter of the first medical missionary, Dr. David Metheny. There is an item in the report from Mersine to the Board in 1894, ten years before, to the effect that "the eldest daughter of Dr. Metheny also organized a girls' prayermeeting in the boarding school." At that early age she already felt the 'urge" which finally brought her back to Syria for her life work.

THE LOSSES IN PERSONNEL in this ten years were very heavy. At the very beginning, on June 4th, 1897, Dr. David Metheny ended his eventful life at Mersine. He came to Latakia only four years after the opening of the mission there and his mighty will drove his feeble body to the limit of all the thirty-three years of his foreign ministry. Like his divine Master he could testify "The zeal of thine house hath consumed me." When greatly weakened towards the last and urged to go home to be buried among his own people, his zeal for Syria was apparent in his reply: "No, I wish to be buried right here where I have borne my testimony. I want to get up on the resurrection day and tell those who have rejected my message, 'I told you how it would be'."

Although by profession a physician and surgeon, and most skilful as such, so that on occasion he was paid big fees to go back a day's journey by steamer to Latakia to perform operations, Dr. Metheny so combined preaching with healing that Synod was persuaded to order his ordination when he was home on his first furlough in 1873. And he spent not himself only, but whatever money he possessed to carry on the work to which his life was devoted. A property carefully estimated by a committee appointed by the Board at $25,-000.00 was erected entirely at his personal expense. It housed the two boarding and day schools at Mersine, the persons in charge of them, two missionary families, a small hospital and pharmacy and clinic. He purchased ground and built several less expensive buildings for the schools and the missionaries for the hot season also in Guzne.

Rev. J. B. Dodds and wife, after only five years in the field, were compelled by the illness of Mrs. Dodds to go home for a rest in the autumn of 1898. Miss Cunningham carried on alone at Suadea during their absence. After two years they returned, but were able to remain only three years, when persistent illness of

Mrs. Dodds and their son persuaded them to resign and go home again in 1903. Mr. Dodds came back alone at the close of this decade in 1906 for a two years engagement.

In 1900 Dr. S. A. S. Metheny and family, after only four years in the field, felt constrained to resign also. Several eminent physicians gave the opinion that their little son could never be cured of his malaria while he remained in Turkey. This was a loss deeply felt and deplored by the Mission and the Board, as it left Mersine and that field without a doctor and with little prospect of finding one so well qualified to fill the place as the son of the pioneer medical missionary. But Dr. Metheny did not cease to labor for the Mission as he was soon made president of the Board and served well in that capacity for twenty years after his resignation and return home. He was a man greatly beloved and left a deep impression for good in many hearts.

The Syrian Church suffered a severe loss in 1899 in the death of Mr. Daoud Makhloof. This is the convert from the Alaweets who was tested by cruel hardships and persecutions in the Turkish Army for seven years. He was not allowed to communicate with his friends all that time, so he was given up for dead until he suddenly reappeared after being mustered out at last. He was able to testify with Paul: "I have been in perils by mine own countrymen; in perils among false brethren; in weariness and painfulness; beaten and threatened with death; yet I have kept the faith and there is laid up for me a crown of righteousness which the Lord will give me at that day.' Much could be written of his eventful life. "Born a pagan, saved by the blood of Christ, kept faithful through much suffering," his life is an incentive to greater self denial, courage and loyalty in the service of our Lord.

Miss Willa Dodds, the efficient helper of Dr. Balph in the hospital and clinics at Latakia, was stricken with paralysis in February 1904. She was taken to the home land in the care of Miss Sterrett and Dr. and Mrs. Balph the following May. The latter remained for their furlough but Miss Sterrett returned to Mersine after a short visit with the home folks.

A new station was opened at Alexandretta by the Scotch-Irish Mission in 1902, near the end of this decade. Rev. S. H. Kennedy and wife were transferred there from Antioch and held a church service the very first Sabbath. As soon as the government heard of it police were sent to investigate. On learning they had no permit, as they held the meetings in their own sitting room, they said little to the missionaries but warned each of the seven men who attended that "if you do so again we will lay hands on you." So Mr. Kennedy went off to the capital of the province, Aleppo, the very next day to get a permit both for a church and a school. With proverbial British bull-dog pertinacity he remained right there six weeks until the necessary permits were finally handed over. School was opened there in October, 1903.

Miss Evangeline Metheny came the following year to their help and thereafter gave an excellent account of herself as an educator of the youth and a witness for Christ. She maintained the traditional Metheny propensity for the unusual. She acquired a reputation for learning a new language each time she went on furlough, most of the learning being done on shipboard enroute.

A brief experience with a presbytery, organized in 1895 and disorganized the year following through failure to meet, persuaded the Synod to return to the plan of a commission for presbyterial business in Syria. The first meeting of the new commission was in September, 1898, at Latakia.

There were some sad cases of defection during this decade. One involved a licentiate at Tarsus who had given much promise by years of efficient and faithful service but fell grievously at the last. The other two were elders at Latakia who withdrew from the Church on account of some difference of opinion with the missionary pastor. These both returned later and served the Church and mission faithfully, one of them removing to Egypt and becoming prominent in the work of the Church there.

School attendance in Latakia was affected unfavorably for awhile at the close of the century by the opening of special Russian schools for the Orthodox Greek Church, with a special fund collected in Russia originally for the Holy Sepulchre in Jerusalem. The new school "swept clean" at first, tempting two of our best teachers away from us by higher wages, and by the activity of the priests taking many of our pupils away also. But this is one of the benefits of opening a mission school. It causes the opening of other schools in competition and thus a larger number are educated. The better class of parents soon found their children were not doing so well in the new school, so attendance increased again in ours. Even non-Christians have often testified to the superior results obtained in our schools, especially in morals.

Village schools in the south of our field, at Tartoos, Melky, Soda and Bizak were well attended. In the Alaweet villages some visits were made but no regular schools could be held. Many of the mountain children were brought to the boarding schools in Latakia, however. An average of about six hundred and fifty pupils in the whole field were under definite Christian instruction, of whom two hundred and fifty were boarders.

Every missionary who has had experience in conducting both boarding and day schools, testifies to the vastly superior satisfaction they found in the influence of the boarding school. Six such were open in this period; one for boys and one for girls at each of the three stations, Latakia, Suadea and Mersine. Most of the children accepted as boarders in those days were practically orphans, and would have had no schooling if we had not provided for them. Indeed many of them had no place worthy to be called a home. In these boarding schools a real Christian home was provided for them. Every pupil in them had to read and study the Bible every day, besides committing large numbers of Bible verses and the catechism—even, in the more advanced classes, the formidable Larger Catechism with proofs. They had morning and evening worship with a blessing at their meals. They were kept under wholesome discipline twenty-four hours a day. They went to Church and Sabbath School and the mid-week prayer meeting regularly. Even their play as well as their study outside of school hours was supervised by competent Christian teachers. No wonder even prominent Moslems said: "We like your schools for their influence on the morals of our children." We are convinced that more spiritual dynamite has been planted in the social structure of Syria by these Christian boarding schools than by any other one method. "My Word shall not return unto me void," saith the Lord.

Medical work was reduced some by the removal of both physicians from Mersine and the one from Suadea. Dr. Balph continued all the period to minister to thousands effectively in Latakia and vicinity in his clinics and hospital and house visits. Miss Meta Cunningham relieved hundreds by her simple ministry for which a short medical course while on furlough had prepared her. But in 1905 she spent the last of her strength in her beloved task and was escorted by heavenly messengers into the rest that remaineth.

Preaching went on regularly in season and out of season at all the dozen or more stations. Accessions for the ten years totaled about three hundred, exclusive of Cyprus which is to be treated separately. Five missionaries and a number of licentiates labored persistently in this department.

The close of this decade marked the jubilee of Covenanter Foreign Missions. A comparison was made at the time in the report of the Board to Synod. In 1856 five denominations had missionaries in the foreign field while in 1906 seventy-six Protestant societies were in the work. Then there were 1369 foreign missionaries while after fifty years there were 11,157. Then there were 180,653 native communicants; in 1906, 1,325,885.

The new accessions in 1906 were almost equal to the total for all the years previous to 1856. This shows great progress compared to previous centuries of Protestant activity.

In this progress we shared as a denomination. Counting all the fields we sent out sixty-eight missionaries in the fifty years. Thirteen passed to their reward before the jubilee. Twenty-two resigned, mostly on account of failing health. One was transferred by marriage to another society. This left thirty-two in the field; six for the Scotch-Irish Church, three at Antioch and three at Alexandretta; eight remained in South China; four in Cyprus; nine in Latakia; three of them just new arrivals; five were at Mersine, two of them just newcomers.

The total accessions for all our fields, as nearly as it seems possible to determine, was about seven hundred and fifty, only about four hundred and fifty of whom remained to celebrate the jubilee with us. Most of the missing were with the Lord. Some, doubtless, were on the other side of the fixed gulf, but very few we hope. Many were dispersed over the face of the earth, in Egypt, Palestine, Europe, the two Americas and the islands. Some of these, we are sure, "went everywhere preaching the Word." It will be a great day when we all meet again around the great white throne to celebrate the greater jubilee.

BOYS' SCHOOL BUILDING, LATAKIA, SYRIA
Girls' school and hospital buildings in the background.

The Sixth Decade, 1906-1916

This period began auspiciously. The Church and the Mission had just been greatly heartened by the celebration of the first half century of our foreign mission effort. But the decade closed with most of the human race suffering under the darkest clouds of calamity that had obscured the light since the days of the Deluge. A single pistol shot in the Balkans in 1914 started a train of fire which exploded most of the bulging war magazines of Europe and plunged the world into the madness of an inferno from which it has hardly begun to recover yet, twenty years afterward. Nay, there are rather many alarming signs of an even more disastrous relapse.

Those who were able to remain at their posts in the Syrian field to the end of this period are:

Rev. J. S. Stewart and wife and Miss Wylie and Miss Edgar at Latakia. Dr. Balph and wife were there also until 1913 when they went home on furlough and were prevented returning until 1919. Miss Patton and the McFarlands remained there also until 1910 when the former resigned to become the wife of Mr. J. D. Edgar, then of Cyprus Academy, and the McFarlands were transferred to Mersine.

Dr. Martin and wife were at Antioch until their furlough in 1914 from which they were not able to return until 1919.

Rev. S. H. Kennedy and wife and Miss Metheny continued to work at Alexandretta until he was arrested and expelled from the country in 1914 as an enemy alien. He and his wife found very fruitful work with the British Y. M. C. A. in Egypt until they were able to return to Syria in 1919. Both seemed to regard this period of exile in Egypt the most fruitful period of their Christian ministry. Indeed all the missionaries who were prevented for any reason from continuing to serve in their chosen field during the war period seem to have found most fruitful service in other fields either at home or on Red Cross or Near East relief in the stricken areas.

At Mersine Miss Sterrett remained through the decade, but Rev. R. J. Dodds and family were forced home by his failing health in 1907 and his brother, Rev. C. A., also resigned in 1910 to take their daughter home for treatment to save her eye-sight. The McFarlands came to Mersine in 1910 to take the place of the Doddses and were able to remain through the period.

Rev. J. B. Dodds completed his two year engagement at Suadea and went home in 1908. He was able to increase interest in the Gospel there very decidedly in that short period by a special plan of evening meetings in the various homes.

Reinforcements in the period were: Rev. Samuel Edgar and wife, Jennie (Faris) Edgar, who came to Latakia in 1907. He had received appointment the year previous but the medical examination discovered a lung condition that made it advisable to postpone his departure. On being examined again a year later however the physician was amazed to find the lung entirely clear, evidence that the Lord had heard the many fervent prayers that had been offered for the removal of this hindrance to his going to his chosen work. He worked at Latakia until his arrest and expulsion in 1914 as an enemy alien, his passport being British. It should be said that in his case and that of Dr. Kennedy, expulsion was the result of vigorous efforts on the part of the American Consul to prevent a worse evil, detention in a concentration camp in the interior of the country. Other Britishers were not so fortunate.

Dr. John Peoples came to Mersine in 1907 and served as a physician there until the end of the war. Miss Evadna Sterrett, Jr., became his helpmeet by marriage in 1910.

Miss F. Elma French joined the force at Mersine in 1907 also and labored with diligence in the schools there with Miss Sterrett until her furlough in 1914, from which she could not return until 1919.

Rev. R. E. Willson and wife, Margaret (Kilpatrick) Willson, reached Mersine in 1908 and went on furlough in 1913, not returning until 1919. Mr. J. F. Carithers came out as a "short termer" to teach English at Mersine near the end of the period, 1913. With difficulty he got away home in 1917 as America was coming into the war.

Miss May Elsey came to serve as head nurse in the Latakia hospital in 1908 where she did most efficient service until her marriage in 1913 to the talented pharmacist and assistant to Dr. Balph, Mr. Sadik Fattal. Miss Louise Crockett came in 1910 and taught four years in the Girls' School at Latakia.

Miss Florence Mearns of Seattle came to teach in Latakia in 1913 but remained only until 1915 when school work was so much restricted by the war that she felt she was no longer needed there.

Until the war the schools were in a more prosperous condition than in former periods. As many as 75 boarders and 200 day-pupils were attending the two Mersine schols, while the day school at Tarsus attracted about 60 more, mostly from the Alaweets.

The new school at Alexandretta, although requiring from the first the payment of reasonable school fees, grew steadily in numbers and in influence. Antioch and Suadea also had a goodly number under instruction although Suadea was without a missionary to direct the work after the departure of Rev. J. B. Dodds in 1908, except for occasional visits by some of the Latakia contingent. Each such visit meant four days' weary riding on horse or muleback over rough mountain trails through a region where very little Arabic was spoken.

At Latakia the two schools took care of about 100 boarders and about the same number of day pupils. Miss Edgar mothering the boys and Miss Wylie, with the aid of Miss Patton for a few years, looked after the girls. Until 1910 four outside schools gave opportunity to the country boys to learn to read the Book of Books, and about 150 took advantage of it. But in 1910 the new political conditions encouraged the Mission to open seven more schools in Alaweet villages which increased the outside attendance to about 300.

These changes were wrought by the adoption of a constitution in 1908 when a bloodless revolution led by the Young Turks, Enver Pasha and Kamil Pasha, with most of the army in support, "persuaded" the frightened old tyrant, Abdul Hamid, to issue the necessary royal decree and form a new cabinet with Kamil Pasha at its head and a prominent young Greek Orthodox Christian with an Armenian and the Sheikh El Islam as associates.

But although the revolution itself was bloodless, the new government was confronted with many outbreaks of disorder in various places, incited by reactionary Turks, both official and civilian with the old Sultan himself, in all probability, as chief conspirator. The worst of these disturbances so far as Protestant missions were affected, was the Armenian massacre of 1909 with its indescribable horrors of barbaric brutality and destructiveness, when the new promise of civil liberty was less than a year old. Here is "how it feels to be massacred in Turkey," as told by an eyewitness, then a boy of fifteen, now our faithful pastor at Inkzik. He says:

"On the morning of April 14, 1909, when going with my father as usual to the market in Adana, we were stopped by a policeman who ordered us back to our homes. We soon found the streets were being cleared and all the places of business were closed, so all Christians were soon in a panic of fear and rushing about frantically hunting for a place of refuge. This panic was increased as the firing of rifles was soon heard in all parts of the city. But that first day was largely given up to the looting of the shops and tearing the wooden parts from the deserted stone houses, for lumber is valuable. The murderous hordes brought in from the mountains for the ugly business must collect their pay before they would begin the business in earnest.

But the second morning blood began to flow as each place of refuge was attacked and the inmates slaughtered, men, women and children. About five hundred had gathered in our little yard and we kept the gate locked and waited, lifting up our hearts to God to protect us. We did not have to wait long until we saw a great crowd of the savage mountaineers, *led by a policeman,* coming in our direction, armed with rifles and tools for breaking up the houses and shouting: 'Hurrah for Mohammed.' As two or three of our party had shot-guns with them they fired them as the crowd rushed at our gate. The effect was amazing. The whole crowd turned and fled. Soon another crowd of the same kind approached with the same result. So we spent the whole of that day, hearing the screams of our neighbors as they were caught and killed, and watching the smoke from their burning homes. At dark some proposed we leave our refuge and go to one of the churches, but we decided it was too far to be safe, although the fire was threatening to reach us and compel us to go.

"The first light of the third day showed us we were surrounded by crowds of the savage killers who at once rushed again to the attack, but again showed no stomach to face even the fire of a couple of shotguns, and so they fled in confusion. Others came in succession and were driven off until towards noon a large reinforcement *of soldiers* came to help them and the bullets began falling upon us thick and fast. A woman of our crowd was wounded and kept up such a continual screaming that she drove the rest of the women frantic, so they rushed to the gate to escape from what seemed to them a death trap and before they could be stopped they had it open and rushed out in the face of the rifle fire. The rest of us followed of necessity and about fifty were killed right there, and indeed all met the same fate who ran towards the city, but it was our good fortune to turn in another direction where we found refuge in some deserted and looted houses. After a few more hours of this inferno, orders were issued by the government that the massacre should stop, and stop it did at once. But after gathering all the guns from the surviving Armenians the second massacre began, which was worse than the first.

"During the interval of nearly a week the survivors of the first killing had gathered, mostly in the churches, since their homes were in ruins. Now these churches were set on fire and as the people were forced to flee from them they were ruthlessly shot down. We were forced from one church in that way but reached another by the good hand of our God upon us. Here the fire was about to reach us also when the crowd of soldiers broke in and took us all prisoners, marching us off to an open space on the riverside where we were told we were to be shot and our bodies thrown into the river. But here again the Lord took a hand and we found our captors were divided. Part of them were of the liberty party and favored sparing us, and finally prevailed on the others and we were marched to a German factory and lodged in its large yard where we remained in hunger and weariness until order was restored and relief measures gave us another lease on life."

Similar scenes were enacted in many other places so that relief operations occupied most of the time of the missionaries at Adana, Alexandretta, Latakia, and elsewhere for many weeks afterward.

The escape of our brethren at Gunimea was a marked answer to the prayers offered in their behalf. The horde approached in sight of the village and our people all fled to the recesses of the mountains, while the party debated the matter of an attack, and at last marched away leaving the village untouched.

These 1909 massacres, which snuffed out the lives of about 40,000 of the best people of Turkey and carried hundreds of their daughters into forced marriages with the murderers of their parents and left about 200,000 homeless and destitute, seem to have been the dying spasms of the reactionary forces opposed to the operation of the new constitutional government. So in 1910 we find our missionaries taking heart again and pushing out with their scholars into the almost forbidden regions heretofore, the Alaweet race. Seven new schools were opened that year in the Latakia Alaweet district. And an increased attendance was reported, largely of Alaweets at Tarsus but more especially of Armenian refugees in Alexandretta and Antioch.

The Alaweets themselves cooperated in the opening of these new schools among them by providing at their own expense a room for the school and in which the teacher and his family could live. True, this was not an ideal arrangement, by American standards, but most of our human endeavors are only efforts in the direction of an ideal. And the house furnished was usually much better than the worst home in the village and almost as good as the best. And as a school it was "the best they had ever seen." Which shows some progress.

The increased number of pupils from the survivors of the massacres would surprise one not knowing the Armenian. It seems that like the fabled Phoenix he rises from the very ashes of his ruined home and looks about for a Christian school for his children and denies himself to the verge of starvation to pay the school fees demanded that his children may be properly educated.

Regular preaching was maintained at Mersine, Tarsus, and Adana by Rev. C. A. Dodds until 1910, and then by Rev. A. J. McFarland and Rev. R. E. Willson after Mr. Dodds and family left for home. They were ably helped in this branch of the work by Evangelist Hanna Besna at Adana and Evangelist Michael Luttoof at Tarsus. The latter was successful in disseminating the truth in an informal way through a reading room he conducted through the week. Both these Syrian helpers had the happy gift of being able to get into conversation with men anywhere and everywhere and then turn the talk to things of the Spirit.

In the new station at Alexandretta Dr. Kennedy kept up a preaching service to an increasing number of members and adherents. But when Turkey joined Germany in the war against Britain and her allies in 1914, Dr. Kennedy, being British, was arrested and held for a little time along with other Britishers, and the allies were given notice that if Alexandretta was bombarded and any Turkish lives were lost, the lives of Dr. Kennedy and his fellow prisoners would be forfeited. But by the intercession of the American consular authorities he was finally allowed to leave the country by the port of Mersine, and found refuge in Egypt. Mrs. Kennedy soon followed him thither and together they had a most interesting work among the British soldiers in the British Aımy Y. M. C. A. in Alexandria. While visiting the wounded Tommies in the hospital there one day, she found a man who seemed to be suffering a great deal. On entering into conversation with him she learned he was from Airdrie and she said: "I have been in Airdrie." His face brightened up at once and he said: "Do you know Rev. J. McDonald?" On learning she did, he begged her to write to Mr. McDonald and ask him to send him some Airdrie newspapers. Not long after, she visited him again and found the bed rail both at the head and foot just covered with newspapers, and the nurse in perplexity, as he would not allow her to remove one of them even. He lived to get back to his beloved Airdrie. Many other stories of her experiences ended less happily. Dr. Kennedy felt he did some of his most effective preaching to those homesick soldiers in those dark years of the war.

Dr. Martin, the pioneer missionary of the Irish Church to Syria, continued preaching to the group at Antioch and also about once a year to the smaller group at Idlib, which was a two days' ride on horseback from Antioch. He was fortunate in getting out of the country as soon as the war started and before the ports were closed. He and has family were in Ireland during those sad years. Although well equipped for medical work, Dr. Martin early became convinced that the definite preaching the Gospel in the usual way was the only proper work of a Christian missionary. In 1909 he suffered the loss of his mountain summer home at Kessab which was burned by the mob which raided Kessab and tried to massacre the inhabitants.

Mr. Stewart, who became Dr. Stewart in 1910 by act of Geneva College and also moderator of Synod the same year on furlough, was active in preaching at Latakia, with about two trips a year to Suadea which took two days each way, and about the same to Tartoos, two days horseback ride also in the other direction, and more frequent trips to the nearer villages where we had groups of members. He was able to remain until the end of this decade, notwithstanding the war.

Rev. Samuel Edgar ably assisted Dr. Stewart in this work, especially in the villages, after he had acquised sufficient of the new "brogue" to make himself understood. But being a Britisher he too was arrested early in the war and only by the good offices of the American consul was he saved from a concentration camp in the interior and allowed to embark for Boston. His family soon followed him thither and they remained in the States most of the war years. On one of his village trips he had his leg broken by a kick from a horse as he allowed his own mount to press in to a spring on the way to drink.

Dr. Balph, with Miss Elsey's aid for five years of the period, rendered medical aid to as many as 7700 patients a year, at Latakia.

Dr. Peoples was getting started in medical work at Mersine and Tarsus after a strenuous initiation at Adana, cleaning up after the brutal butchering perpetrated there in 909. With the aid of German army officials he finally was able to open the small hospital at Mersine as a Red Cross hospital, where he treated a great many, both soldiers and civilians, mainly Turkish soldiers who usually came too late to get much benefit and were carried off by the wagon load, after their bodies had been stripped bare, to be buried. Even such rags were in much demand for the surviving soldiers.

A specially sad feature in the closing of this decade for the Latakia group was the passing of the veteran teacher and Bible woman, Miss Mattie R. Wylie, who died in 1916 after a long period of intense suffering from cancer which she endured with such patience as made it in some ways the most effective testimony of her whole life. Having suffered with Christ she now reigns with Him.

A total of about 300 more names were added to the various church rolls, bringing the total for the R. P. Church in Syria to 1050.

Boys' School Building, Latakia, Syria

The Seventh Decade, 1916-1926

Life for Christians, and especially Armenian Christians, was hard enough in Turkey under the Sultan, but the hardships were increased and intensified many fold when to the cruelty of the Sultan was yoked the thoroughness of the Kaiser. Many learned to outwit the Turk and escape much of the cruelty, but they found the Germanized Turk an entirely different proposition. So when the Turco-German council of war decided the Christians in Turkey were a menace to the success of The Central Powers and should be eliminated, Turkish Christians found themselves in an iron grip they had never felt before. For the Armenians it meant wholesale and ruthless deportation and for most of them, ultimately, death by slow starvation or by a more humane method, massacre by their own neighbors. Deir Ez-Zor, far east in the Syrian desert, was the final destination of many, which was reached by slow, torturing trek. Women with small children and babies, some born on the way, often were compelled by their rough soldier escorts at the point of the bayonet to leave their little ones to die by the roadside or were left, when too exhausted to go farther, to die with them and become food for the hungry vultures which followed the caravan. The few who at last reached Deir Ez-Zor were mostly destroyed by the people of the place as vermin, so the place became known as the "Graveyard of the Armenians." The Presbyterians have opened a Mission there since the war. Thus a spiritual oasis has been opened in that place of desert and death.

Our missionaries with hearts rent by the scenes of suffering they were compelled to witness without being able to prevent, did what they could to alleviate Many of the poor victims of ungodly ambition, when long, cruel apprehension was at last turned into reality and the order was given them to go, hastily brought some of their goods to be stored at the Mission. Some were supported through the long agony of waiting for peace by small remittances made to them by the missionary from the proceeds of the sale of such goods, a little at a time, not to attract notice of the officials who were scouring the country to obtain food for the voracious armies.

Mr. McFarland made a special trip to Adana and called on the governor of the province to have our evangelist, Hanna Besna, exempted from the order and was promised that if it was found he was not an Armenian, as we maintained, he would not be sent. But the unscrupulous chief of police hustled him off with the rest. He was sent to old Kir of Moab and by the help of God found favor in the eyes of his captors and was able to give consolation and instruction to many of his fellow exiles and others, and to return in health after the Armistice, praising God for His loving care of him and his.

Our Gunimea brethren were all deported and their homes were demolished by their Moslem neighbors as soon as they were out of sight. They were not sent so far as some, however, and half of them were able to return. The greatest mortality was among their children. Not enough were left to form a school until a new generation grew up after the war.

All Christians were drafted into the labor corps of the army if they were in the various classes called up. They found life pretty hard, as all the best food and clothing was reserved for the fighting corps. The blockade made it very difficult to feed even the regular troops, so the labor corps and the civilian population were reduced to plain bread and water, almost, with such greens as they could grow or gather from the fields. The death rate was high among these. But it was really marvelous the way the Lord preserved our people, and indeed most of the evangelical Christians. The few who were not exempted in one way or another. were assigned to more favored positions in the service and passed through the ordeal "without the smell of fire upon their garments."

At Latakia many of the Christian young men escaped by taking refuge among our Alaweet people in the mountains where we had conducted schools, and the Alaweets as a body defied the government and were not drafted. The government did not have force enough available to attempt coercion of these Syrian Highlanders. The future pastor of Latakia Church was one of these Christian refugees and the experience was helpful to him in giving him friendly acquaintance with this people.

Many Christian girls were drafted as nurses for the army hospitals and one of the saddest sights of the many sad scenes at Mersine, was that of a whole train of open freight cars full of such girls, being returned to their homes, during the short British occupation, over half of them evidently soon to be mothers, mute testimony to the life they had been compelled to live in that service. Even the war-hardened British Tommies commented on it with a note of horror in the voice.

And what of our missionaries during these years of a darkness that could be felt? Our British friends were hit first and hit hardest. Even their homes were commandeered and used for officers' quarters after the owners were forced to leave them and the country behind them. And little of value that could be easily moved was left in them to welcome them on their return.

On the entrance of the United States into the debacle in 1917 the United States consuls persuaded all the missionaries at Mersine to evacuate except Dr. Peoples and Mr. McFarland. All went home except Mrs. McFarland who remained in Switzerland. She was able to put her talents to good use, dividing her time between the United States consulate and the office of the Near East Relief, located there.

At Latakia, Dr. Stewart and family and Miss Edgar were allowed to remain until he seems to have become the innocent victim of attempts made to communicate with passing intelligence boats of "the enemy" by signal lights from a house back of the dwelling of Dr. Stewart, so suspicion fell on him and he was exiled to Konia, old Iconia, far north in Asia Minor. The overland journey as a prisoner was full of hardships, taking many days on foot or on donkey, with almost sleepless nights in vermin infested prisons. Some relief was furnished when from such a lodging in Tarsus he was able to get the attention of Evangelist Michael, as he passed his window and with the aid of Mrs. Christie of the American Board Mission there, better entertainment was secured for him. At Konia also he found a helpful friend in a lady missionary of that Board, so he was able to have "his own hired house and receive all that came to him." And many came, so he preached to a good audience each Sabbath, and tutored some in English also through the week.

The R. P. Mission force in this field was thus reduced to two very lonely women, Mrs. Stewart and Miss Edgar, at Latakia, and two even more lonely men, Dr. Peoples and Mr. McFarland, at Mersine. Notwithstanding, a large amount of effective work was kept going. Even at Alexandretta, after the exit of the missionaries and the exiling of many of the Syrian helpers, the school was kept going and some church work also, partly by supervision by a local Standard Oil representative who had become a great friend of the Kennedys, and with a visit of a week and some distant supervision by Mr. McFarland. But even the Standard Oil man had to go after a time and the way was closed between there and Mersine.

Schools of the Mersine Mission were kept going with some increase in attendance at times, but part of the time towards the last the schools in Mersine had to be removed to the teachers' homes, as the government anticipated orders any day to take over our buildings for officers' quarters. Even our church services had to be removed to the home of one of the members, although the threat was never really executed. Dr. Peoples continued in charge of the hospital but at the last it was in practical control of the German officer and none but soldiers could be admitted. But as many as a hundred beds were furnished and filled by the many poor victims of Turco-German oppression who dragged their weary way on foot from the labor corps where they had sickened, and arrived often too exhausted and too late to be benefited by our efficient doctor and his capable Armenian nurse.

Preaching was continued by Dr. McFarland at Mersina with an occasional visit of supervision and inspection and to hold communion at Tarsus and Adana. Evangelist Michael was allowed to continue his excellent ministry at Tarsus all the time.

Much temporal and moral relief was furnished by these four missionaries to the half famished women and children from whom their bread winners had been dragged into the insatiable war machine. As many as 250 were on the accepted list of recipients at Mersine, which was favored with a monthly grant from the Relief office in Switzerland where Mrs. McFarland assisted part time.

Although some of our American mission property was occupied for war or government purposes it was not plundered, owing to the presence of some of our missionaries in the vicinity. To head off a worse occupation that was threatening, a young German battery officer, who was known to be looking for suitable quarters at the time, was invited to take up quarters along with Mr. McFarland in the McFarland home. This proved a very pleasant and helpful arrangement and the two "enemies" got on fine together until the officer was transferred to the south to help try to stop General Allenby. There were two memorable incidents of this association.

One evening when playing crokinole together it occurred to the officer to take a snapshot of the act by arranging a flash with a time fuse so he could return to his place at the board before it flashed. The resulting picture was good and the copy given to the missionary was sent to his wife in Switzerland. In all innocence and in her joy at getting it she showed it to the consul whom she was assisting. He took a look at it and then after a second look exclaimed: "Why this is just what we have been wanting. The uniform on that officer tells us there is a German battery at Mersine." Mrs. McFarland's joy was turned to alarm and she begged the consul not to reveal how he got the information.

Sometimes hydroplane officers were entertained at tea by this battery officer which he always insisted Mr. McFarland should share. They regaled us with stories how they had been over the harbor at Cyprus the previous morning and dropping bombs on the British shipping there. And they were actually seen attempting to blow up an "enemy" scout boat which nosed into the Mersine roadstead to see what it could see, soon saw enough and quickly turned and zig-zagged off towards Cyprus with bombs from the plane making visible splashes in the sea quite close to it, but none hitting.

Another day it came back ready for such antagonists and responded to the bombs with shots which frightened the plane to go so high it could aim less accurately and when at last the plane came down near shore the shots came splashing after it so the pilot quickly jumped out and rushed wading through the water to a place of refuge on the land.

Brooding on all the dastardly business of the war as suggested by such scenes and seeing from his window two of these planes taking off on some mission one morning, the missionary cried out from his very soul: "Lord, destroy their machines but save the men."

The next morning Dr. Peoples reported that one of these planes had been demolished when in landing it struck the roof of a house near the shore and capsized, the pilot escaping. In the evening the other plane found the water so rough when it landed that it sunk and was lost, the pilot also escaping by swimming ashore. "Coincidence," says the skeptic. Yes, a striking coincidence, like that of a bullet striking the mark when it has been aimed by an experienced marksman.

At long last the sweetest word that could fall on the ears of a war weary world, fell on our ears one night in November, 1918, when hearing some disturbance in the city and calling down to one passing as to the cause, he replied: "Sulh," peace.

Soon the exiles were returning, those who survived, Armenians, soldiers and missionaries. Of the latter, Dr. Stewart reached home first, about New Years, 1919. Mrs. McFarland got back in March of that year. Then Dr. Balph, Miss Sterrett, Miss French, and Mr. and Mrs. Willson, all in Near East uniform, came along a little later. It was thought best for them to sign up with the Relief Society and wear its uniform for protection until the country was in a more settled condition. Then their main work was relief for sometime.

Dr. and Mrs. Kennedy soon arrived at their mission from Egypt. Dr. and Mrs. Martin and Miss Metheny followed not long after.

Miss Metheny and Miss Mearns and Rev. S. Edgar had come out to Palestine with the Red Cross in March, 1918, just after General Allenby had ended the many hundred years of Turkish misrule in that land of sacred memories. Mr. Edgar was able to visit Latakia in that capacity even before Dr. Stewart got back, and give them some of his good cheer and also some more material cheer for those in need of it.

The Board generously offered furloughs to all the workers who had spent the war years in the field, but none accepted until a year later, when the others were better able to carry on alone.

Of the ninety-nine members of the Church in the Mersine Mission all but thirteen were in evidence when the new era of peace began. Not one was missing on account of the deportations or war experiences or defection. In the Latakia Mission the losses by the deportations were heavy. Nearly one hundred of the two hundred eighty-seven members were missing, most of whom had died as a result of the cruel deportations. We wonder if the ex-royal exile at Doorn is never afflicted with visions of the myriads of innocent victims his unrighteous ambition sent to early graves, over the vigorous protests (it is known) made to him by veteran missionaries of his own race who had spent their lives in carrying the Gospel to the Armenians.

The staff of workers in our sister mission of the Scotch-Irish Church was strengthened by the return to the field of Dr. Martin and family in 1919 accompanied by the Rev. William Lytle. Mr. Lytle entered the language school in Souk-el Gharb for three years of hard study. Later he took up the work in Antioch on the retirement of Dr. Martin. In 1923 he was united in marriage with Miss Agnes Archer, missionary in Latakia. Under their leadership the work in Antioch has made marked progress.

The Synod of 1920 devised liberal things for Foreign Missions—too liberal, as it proved, to be maintained. The high elevation of Greeley where Synod met, the presence in the moderator's chair of a survivor of the war years in Turkey, Andrew J. McFarland, and the general exaltation of the churches which produced the extravagant Inter-Church World movement, probably all contributed to the result, which was no less than $105,000 as the year's budget for Foreign Missions alone, and $1,250,000 as a five year budget for all the work of the Church. And $75,000 was actually contributed that year for Foreign Missions with $50,-000 additional for the home work. Little wonder some began to cry: "Foreign Missions is breaking the back of the Covenanter Church." But as the Negro preacher reminds us, Church backs are not broken that way. He told his people: "Whenever this Church dies from too much givin', I wants to preach its funeral sermon, and 'dis am my text: 'Blessed are the dead which die in the Lord.

Late in 1919 Rev. Wm. Lytle came out from Ireland to get ready to take over the work at Antioch. He spent two years in language school where he made an enviable record in acquiring the language. But he probably regards his most valuable acquisition in those years, his winning a wife in the person of Miss Agnes Archer who came out as a nurse in 1922 from Philadelphia and was in the school preparing for work at Mersine. He was the third minister to come out to the Antioch Mission without a wife and the third to supply that deficiency from among the belles of the Latakia Mission. After their marriage in 1923 they spent one year in Suadea, which had been turned over to them by our Board in 1922. But on the retirement of Dr. Martin in 1924 they were transferred to Antioch.

In tendering his resignation in 1924 after fifty-two years as a Syrian missionary Dr. Martin reported that he could point to one hundred and seven persons as the fruit of his labors in that period.

Miss M. K. Cunningham came from Ireland to their Mission in 1920 also, and has labored faithfully and fruitfully in school work at Antioch since that time.

Miss M. E. G. Houston of the Irish Church had a very short period of service, coming out in 1921 and being transferred to the heavenly service in the summer of 1923, just after completing her course in the language school. But like Samson she may have accomplished more in her beautifully impressive death than in her life.

Dr. R. E. Smith and his wife, Mrs. Jean Shuman Smith, came to Syria in 1921 to assist Dr. Balph in medical work at Latakia.

Miss Lillian Cunningham came to Latakia in 1922 to be head nurse in the hospital where she labored ably and skilfully for five years, the period for which she had contracted.

In the last year of the decade, 1926, Miss Rhea J. McElroy arrived at Latakia to help her sister in the Girls' School.

Of those who were in the field during the war and went on furlough in 1920, Dr. Stewart and wife did not return, but found a similar work among the Syrian immigrants at New Castle, Pa., to whom he ministered for a number of years. He and our Syrian Mission began life the same year, so he too celebrates his 80th anniversary in 1936.

Dr. Peoples and wife were not able to return, owing to sickness both in Mrs. Peoples and their son David which persisted until both of them were translated to "the rest that remaineth."

Miss Edgar delayed her furlough until 1921 and on her return the next year she was transferred to Bible work among women, in which she labored fervently and faithfully the rest of her life. She was able to report the very first year more than a score of moslem homes to which she was welcomed.

Rev. S. Edgar resigned in 1921, turning over the Boys' School and the village work to Rev. A. J. McFarland and wife on their return from their furlough, as they had been transferred to Latakia from Mersine. He had accomplished a good work of reconstruction after the war and had the joy of sharing in the installation of a Syrian pastor in the Latakia congregation before he left. It was a hard tug on his heart strings to give up the Syrian work, but the Lord seemed so to order it.

The McFarlands had the good fortune to take over the Boys' School at a time when there was a great awakening in Syria as to the benefits of an education and before the government was able to do much in meeting this demand. Mrs. McFarland was able to give full time as a teacher of English and to take entire charge of the boarding department. The congregation now having a Syrian pastor, Mr. McFarland was able to concentrate more on the school work also. As a result some of the Syrian leaders expressed the opinion that in this period the school enjoyed its golden age. Two of its graduates were able to qualify without further help for entrance into the freshman class of Beirut University. Three others, after a study of theology under Mr. McFarland and others, were licensed to preach. Five became acceptable teachers in our mission schools.

The year 1922 was one of new calamities for our

Tarsus Mission. When the French were driven from that region by a revived Turkey under the remarkable leader, Mustupha Kemal Pasha, and later a Greek army of invasion suffered the same fate, Christians who were not forcibly expelled felt that the time had come to escape from a land where they had suffered almost annihilation. The poor harassed remnants of the Armenians were the first to leave their pitiful efforts to rebuild on the ruins of the homes to which they had so recently returned from the former exile. Some fled to Cyprus and some to Egypt but most of them crowded into various cities of Syria, following the fleeing French army thither. They well-nigh overwhelmed the French Mandate authorities there, who attempted to save them from starvation and exposure.

All but eighteen of our brethren of the Tarsus Mission fled with the rest. Some of them came to Alexandretta and Latakia and remained in our Church. But many were dispersed among other Protestant churches in Beirut, Damascus, and elsewhere.

One lone German woman, now associated with our Antioch friends, led out a thousand orphan children in a long trek of many days through snow storms and mud to the coast where they could embark for safety. Mr. and Mrs. McFarland had been in charge of some three hundred of these orphans just before going on furlough, as the relief authorities made an urgent plea to our Mission for some temporary help.

But the climax of our sorrow was reached when a telegram brought the heart stabbing news that our beloved associate, Rev. R. E. Willson, of Mersine had succumbed to the long fight he had waged to aid in the embarking of the 60,000 of the miserable refugees who passed through Mersine to take ship for other lands. After a short illness from the dreaded Typhus, contracted while ministering to some of the poor victims of Turkish oppression, he passed on to the land "where the wicked cease from troubling and the weary are at rest." Mrs. Willson and the children made their sad way back to the home-land they had left only three years before.

Miss Elma French was now left alone at Mersine with the few who had not fled with the crowd. Confronted by these conditions the Board and many of the missionaries were persuaded that the work of our Mission should now be concentrated in Syria and that Miss French should be transferred to Latakia. But she contended so persistently and earnestly against it that she was allowed to remain, and was able to conduct an interesting Bible work there for many years. She was cheered by only an occasional visit from some missionary from one of our other Missions.

Mersine's terrible loss in this catastrophe was a gain for our other stations. Rev. Michael Luttoof and Teacher Michael Madany were a welcome reinforcement to the work at Alexandretta. Rev. Hanna Besna and son, Teacher Ibrahim Besna, found places to render good service in Latakia.

The Latakia congregation was definitely organized and Pastor Khalil Awad was installed there on May 6, 1921. A few years later, in 1924, a fine church building was erected and dedicated for them, entirely free of debt, from money collected at various times during many years both from Syrians and friends in America by Miss Mattie Wylie and Mrs. J. S. Stewart. The work was actually undertaken and carried through under moral and material stimulus from another woman missionary, Mrs. McFarland. The Lord's hand was manifested impressively in saving the fund from a fatal loss through a sudden and severe drop in Syrian exchange just then. Usually Mission money came to Beirut from America and was at once converted into Syrian money and deposited to our account. As we knew this money had come and suposed it had been deposited in the usual way, we were appalled to hear of the frightful drop in Syrian exchange, and many were ready to give up the project of building. But on writing to Beirut we were lifted to heights of joy and gratitude to learn that just before getting this money the plan of deposit had been changed, so our credit had been made in dollars and we suffered no loss.

The medical department, strengthened by the coming of Dr. Smith, treated an increased number of patients, reaching in one year 15,000. But Dr. Balph's failing health led him to resign the last year of this decade and he and Mrs. Balph returned to America. She had given of her best, which was most excellent, for the long period of forty-five years, following the noble example of the first woman "who ministered to Christ." Doctor had served thirty-nine years and was given a most affecting farewell on his departure, in which Moslems vied with Christians of all sects in assuring him of their deep appreciation of his fine ministry to their bodies and their souls, and their great heaviness of spirit at the prospect of separation from him. Dr. Balph did not long survive that separation, entering his rich eternal reward September 7, 1926.

Faithful preaching of the Word was continued by all the ministers and evangelists, through all the years of the war and the tragic disturbances that followed. But accessions fell off some. Only about two hundred were received in all the stations during the ten years.

Schools were kept going and many new ones reopened, so that twelve village schools with about 350 pupils were reported in 1926. About 500 more were receiving advanced education in the several city schools of the Missions, the Irish and the American.

The Board, the Foreign Missions and every individual missionary was keenly sensible to an irreparable loss in the going home "like a shock of corn fully ripe" of that Generalissimo of Foreign Missions, Dr. R. M. Sommerville, who had served so whole-heartedly and untiringly and sympathetically for so many years in the highly important office of Corresponding Secretary of the Board, the second only to occupy that office, Dr. S. O. Wylie being the first. He left us for the eternal fellowship of the saints in glory February 3, 1920.

The Eighth Decade, 1926-1936

DEPRESSION

The last decade of our story is in its most prominent feature, a period of depression. Instead of expansion we have a story of retrenchment due to the steadily decreasing appropriations from the home church. This involved painful readjustments but as missionaries were retired new efforts were put forth to tap unused resources within the field itself. All missionaries and Syrian co-workers suffered two salary cuts of ten per cent each time and an even heavier loss in exchange due to the devalued dollar. The village schools took the brunt of the retrenchment financially. Four of them, all in Alaweet villages, were closed.

Our Scotch-Irish brethren suffered also from the fall in Sterling in which their salaries are paid, but their Board made up to them part of this loss, and their Syrian associates were paid on the gold basis for which reason they did not suffer so much as the workers in our part of the field. But there has been surprisingly little complaint from our fellow workers on account of these successive cuts. The Lord who kept the widow's oil from failing in order to feed His servant Elijah, has found ways to provide for all His servants in Syria in this extremity also. Jehovah-Jireh is His name. We have not been unmindful of the fact that where the work in Syria was once the sole foreign missionary interest of the Covenanter Church in America, work on a correspondingly large scale has been developed in three other fields, so we have to be content when we receive a fair share of the church's contributions for foreign missions.

HOSPITAL CLOSED

The Latakia mission hospital, opened by Dr. Balph in 1896, was closed in 1934. Early in this decade a well equipped and well staffed county hospital was opened in Latakia by the government. For four successive years, before the new hospital began to operate fully, the treatments at our hospital and clinics averaged eleven thousand a year, but for the last six years the number of treatments declined to two thousand a year. That means about six a day including those seen by the physician in the free clinics, the hospital, or in their homes. In face of such competition the decision to close the hospital was fully justified. This meant the ending of medical mission work in Syria. It was with real regret that we saw the passing of an institution which had made such a notable contribution to human well-being. Though it had fulfilled its mission, its ministry long will be remembered. Dr. and Mrs. Smith returned home and entered work in Los Angeles, California, but the work in Syria still has a large place in their hearts.

MISS EDGAR'S TRAGIC DEATH

One of the heaviest blows that has fallen on the Mission in all its history fell on January 25, 1932, when Miss Maggie B. Edgar failed to return from a visit to a non-Christian home to which she had gone in her Bible work. Although she had obtained the consent of the Board to retire some years before, with the privilege of living in Syria and working only as she felt able, she really continued to serve as a full time worker in her beloved task of carrying some gospel light to her benighted sisters of city and village in Syria, until "she was not, for God took her."

There is plenty of circumstantial evidence to indicate that she was foully murdered by the man of the house where she made her last visit, and near which she was last seen in the flesh. The man is known to have other blood on his soul. It is "whispered" that a woman of the family cried out as Miss Edgar entered that day: "Oh Miss Edgar, why did you come now? My brother will kill you." But the man roughly silenced her saying, "Shut up or I'll cut your tongue out first," and then sank his knife in Miss Edgar's breast. The government made arrests and seemed to exhaust all means available to obtain some direct evidence, but without success. "Precious in the sight of the Lord is the death of his saints."

CHANGES IN PERSONNEL AND POLICY

The Board departed from precedent in 1928 in sending out a married layman, Mr. Chester T. Hutcheson and his wife, Mrs. Ada (Wilson) Hutcheson, both of whom had been short termers in Cyprus, to take charge of the Boys' school in Latakia. Another precedent was abandoned in 1933 when the Hutchesons went on furlough and a Syrian, "Mr. Hanna Madnay, who had been head teacher for many years, was appointed principal of the Boys' school and has served in that capacity quite efficiently ever since. Mr. Hutcheson was returned to the field as director of all the educational work of the Mission and to be business manager of the mission properties. He took over the direction of the Girls' school in place of Miss Elizabeth McElroy who was transferred to Bible work among women. This arrangement too has left the minister-missionary free to devote his whole time to more direct evangelistic effort.

Miss McElroy deserves special credit for opening a flourishing kindergarten department in the Girls' school some years ago which has become financially the most lucrative part of the school, not only paying its own expenses but contributing substantially to the expense of the other departments. Before beginning her new work among women she took courses in a Bible school in Los Angeles. She has entered on this new work with great zeal, which she began on her return from furlough in 1935.

The Rev. Herbert A. Hays and wife, Mrs. Evelyn (Link) Hays, came out in the fall of 1935 to work in Latakia province. After two years of study in the language school in Jerusalem they will take up active work among the Alaweets. The McFarlands, who at the close of this eighth decade completed thirty years in the service of the Mission, will then retire. Thus the permanent staff of missionaries which numbered ten in 1906 and twelve in 1907 will then number only five.

In 1932 Miss French, who had bravely carried on alone in Mersine, was transferred to Idlib, Syria, a station of the Scotch-Irish Mission. Here under the direction of Dr. S. H. Kennedy, she did a valued piece of work in the school and among the women of Idlib. But, as it proved, her life work was nearly done, for after a little more than two years there she passed to her rich reward on April 25, 1935. A Syrian Bible woman and a Syrian Bible man continue to dispense gospel light in Mersine.

SCOTCH-IRISH PART OF THE FIELD

Dr. Emily Lytle, who came out from Ireland to open medical work in Antioch where her brother labors, remained only a short time, from August 1927 to January 1931, and most of this time was spent in the language school. She was married soon after her return home.

Miss Muriel Russell, daughter of the Rev. J. Russell, Secretary of the Scotch-Irish Board, came to help in the Alexandretta school in September, 1931, and after the usual term in the language school took up her work there and has carried it on very successfully.

Miss Metheny had been in charge of that school practically since its opening in 1903 as she arrived the next year. When Miss Russell came, Miss Metheny gave herself more fully to evangelistic work in the villages. On account of ill-health she resigned in 1935 but continues to "let her light shine" in the darkened village homes and hearts as her failing strength permits. Endowed with a talent for languages she was able to give her message in Arabic, Turkish, French, or English, all of which were called for in that region of many tongues. In June, 1936, Geneva College bestowed on her the honorary degree of Litt. D.

The Rev. Archibald Guthrie came out from Ireland in 1934 to take over the work in Alexandretta on the approaching retirement of Dr. and Mrs. S. H. Kennedy, who at the end of this eighth period completed forty-one years of service in the Mission. Their Sabbath School has had a phenomenal growth during this period till now it is by far the largest in Syria and has few to equal it in attendance even in America. The report in 1936 showed more than a thousand on the roll and an average attendance of over seven hundred. To Mrs. Kennedy is due much of the credit for this impressive record. She also has the most flourishing Bible women's organization in these parts. We Americans like to remember that Mrs. Kennedy is an American and of the noble family of Dodds. Miss Metheny too is an American and her mother was a Dodds.

SYNOD'S DEPUTATION

In the autumn of 1931 these missions were favored by a visit from Dr. F. M. Wilson, Corresponding Secretary of the Board in America, accompanied by his wife, and Dr. Walter McCarroll, also of the Board, and his wife. This visit was made in response to the urgent request of many of the missionaries, and after the accumulation of a special fund to defray the expenses of the trip. After a tour of Palestine, a thorough itinerary was made of the work in the Latakia field. Hardly a village was passed by in which we had any work. The deputation also included the stations of the Scotch-Irish mission in its visit, the former stations in Cilicia, and our stations in Cyprus. They also participated in a general conference of all the Reformed Presbyterian missionaries in the Levant, which was held in the Lebanon mountains.

Another reason for the coming of the deputation was to study the workings of the native councils which had been set up under the direction of the Board in Syria and Cyprus. Under the pressure of decreasing income the tempo of the transfer of responsibility from the Mission to the Syrian church was hastened. A first educational step was the setting up of a joint council made up of missionaries and elected representatives of the church in Latakia and of village groups of believers. The authority formerly exercised by the Mission was transferred to this Council. The experiment served a useful purpose in the development of a deeper sense of responsibility on the part of the native church for the evangelization of Syria. The basis of cooperative effort, however, did not prove satisfactory to the Syrian members, so the plan was abandoned and the management of the work was entrusted to Synod's Commission in Syria.

MARKS OF PROGRESS

The Latakia congregation reached complete self-support in the fall of 1935. The pastor, the Rev. Khalil Awad, deserves credit for consenting to a reduction of his already thrice diminished salary in order to make this financial independence of the Board for his congregation possible. Another mile post on the road to a Syrian Covenanter Presbytery was reached when a congregation was organized at Gunimea on June 5, 1933, and another at Inkzik on May 17, 1935. Rev. Ibrahim Besna who was licensed April 19, 1930, and ordained March 23, 1934, was made stated supply at Inkzik. Under his leadership the Holy Spirit has produced a real revival of the work there, and by the generous help of friends in America and the fine cooperation of the Syrians at Inkzik a nice new church building has been completed and dedicated to the worship of the true God as directed by the Scriptures.

Mr. Daoud Tannous also was licensed on March 23, 1934, and later became stated supply at Suadia of the Scotch-Irish Mission. That Mission also licensed two young men, Mr. Mishael Madany and Mr. Jameel Tranjan, at Souklouk on August 12, 1935. Mr. Madany is stated supply at Alexandretta. Mr. Tranjan was ordained at Antioch by the same Commission of the Scotch-Irish Church on July 6, 1936, and installed as pastor of the Antioch congregation. The latter received his education at Antioch, Latakia, and in the United Presbyterian college and seminary at Cairo, Egypt. Mr. Madany is a product of the Latakia Boys' school and the private tuition of Dr. Kennedy of Alexandretta, for the most part, in theology. Mr. Tannous also is a graduate of Latakia school, and of the class of theology conducted there by Dr. McFarland with the assistance of the Rev. Khalil Awad.

A Presbytery might have been organized in the Latakia field therefore in 1935 but for the hope that a plan might be found by which one Presbytery could be formed to include both fields.

One of the pleasant fruits of the visit of the Deputation, at once in evidence, was the enlargement and invigoration of the old annual "Workers Conference" which had been confined mostly to the Latakia field. Under the patronage of the Deputation it received a new name, "A Summer School for Christian Workers." And by the importunate efforts of Dr. Smith, Rev. Wm. Lytle of Antioch was at last awakened to a lively interest in it for his field, and he soon became the moving spirit in it. It now meets every year, alternately in Antioch and Latakia. It has been blessed by the Lord with many good results in both fields. By financial help from both the Scotch-Irish and American Churches it was possible to secure prominent evangelists and Christian teachers from other missions, who have been a great help in giving us all new inspiration and incentive. Mr. Lytle soon developed into a powerful evangelist himself and was called to give help in that line in similar conferences in other missions.

A religious revival at Inkzik of the Latakia field seemed to get its start in one of these Summer Conferences. The whole village, which was a frequent source of annoyance to the government because of bloody fights and thieving, has been affected for good and a number have come out boldly on the Lord's side. A nice new church building was dedicated, practically free of debt, on November 15, 1936, at this place. The Inkzik people gave work and money generously, considering their poverty. The total cost was $1,264. Four hundred dollars of this amount was contributed by the people in America; $667 by the Syrians, the rest by the missionaries.

The Board in 1935 appropriated two thousand dollars for the construction of a summer missionary home in the mountains of Slenfe, for which the missionaries who use it pay rent. This was done that the missionaries should not have to outside of the State of Latakia in order to escape the debilitating heat of the town. The two cuts of ten percent together with the still greater reduction effected by the devalued dollar made it impossible for the married missionary to secure the necessary summer home for himself.

The closing of the medical department left a lot of unused rooms on the hands of the Mission in Latakia. So with the approval of the Board a rental department was opened in charge of the Mission treasurer. Seventeen small apartments were fitted up and rented to as many families. The total annual rental received the last year of this decade was about $764. But about half of this amount was spent in remodeling and repairing the apartments. Indeed all of it was spent and more on such operations when we include the complete new bath room installed at the missionary apartment in the Boys' School building and the re-roofing of half of the Girls' School building. But the latter expense was met by a special contribution of $200 to the Board which was sent out for that purpose.

The 30% cut in the franc in September 1936 added to our financial troubles in Syria where the Syrian currency was based on the franc. Coming just on the eve of the opening of the schools to which the school fees are paid in Syrian and with our large rental business also contracted in Syrian, the Missions were assured of some heavy losses. Teachers' wages too were contracted for in Syrian but on their urgent request and on the example of the Government in increasing the wages of their lower-paid employees, the Latakia Mission felt compelled to make some adjustment on the new franc.

Even greater unrest however was caused toward the

end of these eight decades by the new treaty between France and Syria in which all Syria was promised a large measure of independence. While all welcomed the idea of independence, the minority sects were very naturally apprehensive of coming under Moslem control again after the many sad experiences of such control in the centuries of Turkish rule. So there were strikes and riots in the large cities resulting from the efforts of the various factions to secure an arrangement in the new organization most favorable to their particular interests. The status of Protestant missions under the new regime is uncertain, but God disposes while man proposes, and He will not fail nor be discouraged until He hath set judgement in the earth. Our Redeemer is strong.

The repeated emphasis on definite efforts at personal evangelism in the joint summer conferences, which was stressed by special workers from outside our circles as well as by our own leaders, has borne some fruit among the workers, and there is hope that what has appeared is only the first fruits of a great harvest.

Some impression of the work being carried on by the Covenanters in Syria, on the eightieth anniversary of the landing of their first missionaries in the country, may be conveyed by a few figures.

The Scotch-Irish were operating in 1936 churches and schools at Antioch, Alexandretta, Idlib and Suadea. These were served by Dr. and Mrs. Kennedy and Miss Evangeline Metheny who were on the point of retiring, and by Rev. and Mrs. Lytle, the Misses Russel and Cunningham, and Rev. A. Guthrie, missionaries; and by one ordained Syrian preacher, three Syrian licentiates and twenty-two Syrian teachers, eleven men and eleven women, and nine Bible women. Their anual expenditure, not includig salaries of missionaries, was $11,170, counting the pound Sterling at $5.00; of which 30½ % or $3407 was raised locally.

Latakia Mission had churches and schools at Latakia, Gunimea, Inkzik, Jenderea, Elladaney, and Bahamra; the last three mission stations. Schools were conducted also at three other villages and an itinerant evangelist made monthly visits to about fifteen other villages in the south of our field. This work was carried on by Dr. and Mrs. McFarland who were on the eve of retiring, and by Mr. and Mrs. Hutcheson and Miss McElroy, with Rev. and Mrs. Hays in their second year of language school, preparing to enter on the active work soon. Also three ordained Syrian preachers, twenty-one teachers, fifteen men and six women, one evangelist and one Bible woman made up the Syrian contingent of the force. The annual expenditure, except missionaries' salaries, was $8470, of which 39% or $3303 was raised locally, in 1936. This does not include the amount contributed for the Inkzik church building.

There was a noteworthy increase in the attendance at Sabbath School at Alexandretta during this decade. By means of some financial expenditure for prizes for attendance on the part of Dr. Kennedy and the expenditure of a lot of sole leather by Mrs. Kennedy, in smoking out the laggards each week, the attendance reached near to the thousand mark in 1936.

The total day school attendance in the northern mission in 1936 was 625 for their four schools. In Latakia Mission it was 466 for its two city schools and eight village schools.

Accessions to the church in the north for the ten years were 110; and in Latakia field 139, bringing the total in both missions to about 1500 for the 80 years.

But as Dr. Balph so impressively states in closing his "Fifty Years in Mission Work in Syria," to which we are much indebted for materials for this sketch, you cannot tell the whole story in figures. Thousands whose names were never recorded on the church rolls of these two missions were thoroughly indoctrinated in the way of salvation in our schools, and we cannot but believe that most of them lived a much richer life because of it, and that many of them turned at last before their eyes closed in death to that Saviour who assured the thief crucified with Him that his dying confession was accepted.

Certainly in material and intellectual things there is abundant evidence of great progress in the eighty years our mission has served the Syrians. The change of government in 1919 should be credited with a large share in this progress, but the silent working of the Word of Life, introduced in various ways into the minds and hearts of the multitudes whom the missions contacted in these decades, must also have its meed of credit.

The opening of roads and the introduction of motor cars, mostly American, has wrought a revolution in the ease of travel and in the desire to travel. But the persistent influence of our schools, clinics and churches, has wrought an even greater change in the facilities for gaining useful knowledge and the desire for that knowledge. Commendable efforts have been made by the new government to furnish every Syrian child a chance to get some education, but even in the cities the demand is greater than the government can supply. How different from the opening years of the missions when parents had to be persuaded to send their children to our schools by promises of free tuition, free books, free board and lodging and often even free clothes! And that, notwithstanding that ours were the only schools to be found worthy of the name. The epithet, "Unchangeable East," can no more be properly applied to the Near East, at least. The sleeping giant is awaking from his long sleep, and the persistent prickings of the missions' activities have had much to do with that awakening.

There are signs of disintegration in every one of the four ancient religious sects in our mission field, as each one is more or less divided against itself. The absolute power of the priest and the sheikh is no more. The eyes of many have been opened to know that their religious leaders are but men of like passions with themselves. The new wine of the Gospel has been put into these old wineskins and they are threatening to burst. This is most evident in the Greek Orthodox sect which has actually divided under two rival bishops in the Latakia diocese and the one section has declared independence of the patriarch entirely. Another is divided under two hostile secret societies, one of which has not hesitated to resort to assassination to remove a hostile priest even while in the act of ministering in the sacred courts of his church.

The non-Christian sects are divided more along political lines than religious, but they are divided. The coming of the Son of Man has sent a sword into all these resisting bodies. His peace will follow when they submit to Him.

The whole creation groaneth from the impact of that two-edged sword, waiting for its redemption. How long will it be ere it turn to that Balm of Gilead which can heal its deadly wound and give it rest? Even so, Come, Lord Jesus. Come and reign in that land where you were crucified, from which you ascended and to which you have promised to return in glory. Many followers of Paul have planted the good seed in tears; many others have followed Apollos and watered it. All wait for you, Lord, to give the increase.

www.ingramcontent.com/pod-product-compliance
Lightning Source LLC
Chambersburg PA
CBHW060133050426
42448CB00010B/2107
9781935907565